DELTA TEACHER DEVELOPMENT SERIES
Series editors Mike Burghall and Lindsay Clandfield

English is Context

Practical pragmatics for clear communication

Andreas Grundtvig

Acknowledgements

In acknowledgement, I thank my wife Alma, daughter Vanessa, and dog Ronja, who, often perplexed, temporally lost a husband, a father, and a friend to … an ELT book!?!

My mum, who is to blame for my creative mind and personal way of seeing things; by bringing me into this mad world, she is probably my biggest influence.

My friends Hannah Shipman and Gabriel Clark, for their pedagogical feedback and conviction that with this book I was onto something good.

A fist bump to Nick Boisseau of DELTA, for lending a first sympathetic ear to the project; editor Mike Burghall, whose commitment to the project was dangerously contagious; and Christine Cox, for waving her magic design wand.

And finally, regrettably … thanks to the Corona virus, without which my procrastination would never have allowed me to stay the course.

Dedication

I dedicate this book to four friends who not only believed in me as a writer but provided the boot up the backside I needed to get on with it.

Paul Davis, the kindest mad hatter; a beautiful and brilliant mind, whose wicked sense of humour meant being with him was always a delight; Jim Wright, stronger than an ox in so many ways, whose incredible positivity was enviable: he encouraged me to be myself, with the words … 'wacky is goooood!'.

Both of them no longer alive: stolen from us, just as we were beginning to enjoy ourselves.

Then there's wonderful Susan Holden, who encouraged me to revisit the idea of this book, and gave me the impetus to finish it; and my dear friend Bryan Thomas, who told me to write, write, write … but leave philosophy to those who knew what they were talking about!

Thank you:

Professor Jonathan Culpeper for kindly accepting to write the pragmatic Preface on page 6.
David Heathfield for giving permission to quote the charming story of the Ferryman on page 130.

1st edition 1 5 4 3 2 1 | 2024 23 22 21
The last figure shown denotes the year of impression.

All rights reserved. No part of this publication may be reproduced, stored in a retrieval system, or transmitted, in any form or by any means, electronic, mechanical, photocopying, recording, or otherwise, without prior written permission from the publisher.

DELTA Publishing, 2021
www.deltapublishing.co.uk
© Ernst Klett Sprachen GmbH, Rotebühlstraße 77, 70178 Stuttgart, 2021

Editor: Mike Burghall
Cover and layout: Christine Cox
Cover picture: © Alberto Masnovo/Shutterstock.com
Photo pages 29 and 126: © Quality Stock Arts/Shutterstock.com
The drawings throughout *English is Context* are by Alma Visockaitė-Grundtvig
Printing and binding: Elanders GmbH, Waiblingen

ISBN 978-3-12-501742-9

From the author

On my 45th birthday, my wife Alma, who had had enough of chauffeuring me around, signed me up for driving lessons. That didn't just involve practice sessions with an instructor – I also had to attend a course of 12 theory-based lessons.

Child's play, I thought!

I knew most of the signs, had reasonable road sense and, of course, I knew what traffic lights looked like! Red at the top meant stop, green at the bottom meant go, and – as a kind of transitional warning – between the two was amber.

Then, putting theory into practice, I discovered many situations where *context* changed everything:
- If the lights were green but my view was obscured – perhaps by a pedestrian or a traffic jam – I should not simply career ahead because the signal said go!
- If I was approaching the lights at cruising speed – and they were suddenly to change – I should not immediately slam on the brakes to obey.
- And if there was a policeman directing the traffic, I should ignore the lights *altogether* – no matter what they told me to do.

I knew the *order* of the lights and the *rule*, but I still needed plenty of practice before I knew how to respond in different contexts.

And that, I thought, was precisely how language – and language teaching – work!

I have spent much of my teaching career explaining sentence structure – the order and function of words, as well as their individual meaning. It is my job to test my learners' ability to remember these – by setting reading comprehension tests – with multiple-choice questions, matching exercises and gap fills.

But each time I do, I want to award *additional* marks for *alternative* answers which, depending on the context, just might also be possible.

I have met so many learners who, having satisfied the assessment criteria for a given level of language competence, came back after a trip to Britain, America or another English-speaking environment complaining that they were not able to converse in the language that they had studied so painstakingly. They had learnt the words, the meaning and place in a sentence, but what they *didn't* know was how these words behaved in *context*.

What they needed, I thought, was pragmatic competence.

In 2013, I was fortunate to attend a summer school celebrating the thirtieth anniversary of the publication of 'Principles of Pragmatics' by Professor Geoffrey Leech. The author and other specialists in this field delivered a series of lectures on what he defined as: *'how utterances have meanings in situations.'*

Although the course was not intended for language teachers, everything I learnt – I thought – was *extremely* relevant to my own teaching.

As a consequence of that course, I began delivering teacher training workshops on pragmatics in the classroom. Although they were packed with theory, my workshops often ended up with participants sharing real-life examples of how language had surprised them – because of the context.

And there was certainly plenty to share!

From a business meeting – where diplomacy and tact are important to maintain negotiations – to matters of immediate urgency – such as warning a driver of an immediate hazard – our learners need practical help in seeing how *meaning* and *understanding* of language depend on context.

One day, at the end of one of my workshops, a friend – Jack Heyward-Tuck – offered a quiet word of feedback in my ear: *'This is all very interesting, but what we need are practical activities to deal with it in the classroom.'*

He was right, I thought.

As a consequence, I have since then collected activities, and created my own, to share with others in workshops, in my classes and have noticed that:
- resources to help learners understand how language is used in context are indeed scarce;
- perhaps only the bravest resources have attempted to tackle what I consider to be such an important subject.

I hope I have provided a collection of classroom activities that are simple to set up and to let loose on unsuspecting learners – in the hope that *they*, too, will recognise that … *English is context.*

Contents

	Page
From the author	3
Preface	6

Part A — 7

English is Context	7
Speaking in context	9
Writing in context	9
Discourse in context	10
Change in context	11
English in context	12
Communication in context	14
Connotations in context	15
Conversation in context	15
Conversationalists in context	16
Codes in context	17
Speech in context	18
Confusion in context	19
Cooperation in context	19
Politeness in context	21
Connections in context	22
Face in context	23
Face threats in context	24
Face saving in context	25
Impoliteness in context	26
Relevance in context	28
Pragmatics in context	30
Teaching pragmatics in context	30
Learning pragmatics in context	31
Teaching pragmatics in English	31
Learning pragmatics in English	32
References	33
Recommended reading	34

Part B — 35

How are you polite?	36

Chapter One	39
English is context	
Howyis!	40
English by radio	40
In the mood	41
Pick 'n' mix	41
Classroom tickers	42
What do you suppose?	42
Have you Meghan Markled?	43
Taboo in role	43
Dinner date from history	44
Mind your Ps and Qs!	44
Afflicted with sarcasm	45
Thinking outside the box	45
DIY gap fill	46
Circumstantial synonyms	46
Article of faith	47
Swings and roundabouts	47
So there!	48
Word of the year	48
On the slur of the moment	49
Emoji translators	49
Dot dot dot, dash dash dash	50
Hello, goodbye	50

Chapter Two	51
English in context	
Only half the story!	52
Blame it on the boogie	53
Adjacency pairs	54
Windy lifts, *schody* stairs	56
Song lyrics roleplays	57
Roger Irrelevant	58
Larkin' about	59
A word is a word – or is it?	60
Felicitous conditions	61

Contents

Soap bubbles	62
Simply apply dubbing	64
Cannibalistic commas	65
An open book	66
Cumulus corpus	67
I see black for you	68

Chapter Three
Being direct — 69

Here is the news	70
Speakers' Corner	71
Trollhunters	72
Greta's world	73
Literally speaking	74
Clearing the dead wood	75
Tomorrow is yesterday	76

Chapter Four
Being liked — 78

Claiming common ground	79
A royal bastard	80
Donald, Where's Your Troosers?	81
It's no joke!	82
The Ikea effect	83
Age, sex, location?	84
Simile, please!	86
Celebrity agony aunts – and uncles	87
Reports are from Mars, rapport is from Venus	89
Flattery will get you …	90
The Shakespeare hop	92
The heckle therapist	93
Daley Starr	94
Puntastic punters	95
It takes one to know one	96
Comic strip(tease)	97
Hitting the headlines	98

Chapter Five
Being respected — 99

Sorry seems to be the hardest word	100
A guided tour of the news	101
Plain sailing	102
The name of the game	103
The Spaghetti Challenge	104
You are (not) cordially invited …	105
Any kind of *ism*	106
Mincing your words	107
Sofian's game	109

Chapter Six
Being indirect — 110

Ambiguous appraisals	111
An elephant in the classroom	112
Reasons to steer clear	113
Avoidance charades	114
Reading between the lines	115
Mark my words	116
Brutally civil	118
Literally figurative	119
DC Onomatopoeia	121
A taboo U-turn	122
It's gobbledygook to me!	123
Something …	124

Part C — 125

Ways to think – 127
with the learner in mind

Ways to teach – 130
with the teacher in mind

Ways to succeed – 135
with the teacher and the learner in mind

References — 140

From the editors — 141
From the publisher — 142

Preface

In an age of claims about 'fake news', we are sensitive to the idea that the meanings of words may not match 'true reality' (or, more complicatedly, that the words claiming that something is fake turn out to be fake themselves).

Meanings are not simply decoded from words, perhaps via a dictionary.
- For example, the words 'I'm thirsty' could be a true statement that I am in need of liquid refreshment, but they might well mean something else.

If said in a suitable context, they could be acting as a tentative, possibly polite, request for somebody to make me a drink (imagine them being said to a person who is already pouring themselves a drink).

Such cases, indeed, are not special or rare: this is the fundamental stuff of normal interaction, whether spoken or written.

The study of how meanings are constructed and understood in context is the business of *pragmatics*.

Pragmatics, one might say, is the study of what isn't there:
- Other more traditional areas of linguistics – phonology, morphology, syntax and even semantics – focus on physical material, sounds or graphic representations.

Pragmatics focuses on the meanings that are being *implied* by speakers and *inferred* by hearers in context:
- Sometimes those meanings do match the words, but often the matches are partial or non-existent, leading to cases which we might label as hinting, innuendo, tentativeness, irony, sarcasm, joking, teasing … and much more. The way we generate these meanings is not random.

Pragmatics is particularly interested in the underlying principles that explain how certain words in certain contexts can produce certain meanings:
- You wouldn't request a drink if you were not thirsty; by orientating to a pre-condition of the request, the words 'I'm thirsty' provide a strong hint that you are making the request itself in the relevant context.

Some branches of pragmatics investigate how contexts become associated with words themselves:
- The word 'please', for example, is often referred to by British parents as 'the magic word'.
- 'Please' is not simply a polite word: it is associated with making requests, with smoothing the way and getting what you want.

Some branches of pragmatics investigate the nature of those contexts themselves:
- Making a tentative, indirect request like 'I'm thirsty' might go down well in British culture, but certainly not in *all* cultures (Israeli or Polish, for example).
- There, it could be viewed as having a touch of dishonesty and/or being coldly distant, given that you are not saying what you really want: you are not 'giving it straight' – as a friend would.

English, as any language, is infused with its own contexts.

Constructing and understanding meanings in English relies on knowing its pragmatics.

So, sit back and let the expert tour guides take you on an informative and entertaining journey through the wonderful landscape of English and pragmatics in *English is Context*!

Prof. Jonathan Culpeper, author and former Editor-in-Chief of the Journal of Pragmatics

Follow the *English is Context* blog at:
thebirdisaword.org

English is context, given that – to be able to fully understand the meaning of what is said – we need to know both the circumstance and the conditions present at the time of speaking.

> *'Yo soy yo y mi circunstancia, y si no la salvo a ella no me salvo yo.'*
> José Ortega y Gasset [1]

'I am me and my circumstance, and if I don't save that I don't save myself.' With these words, the Spanish philosopher José Ortega y Gasset referred to his role as a participant within the environment of his existence. Although *English is Context* is not a book about philosophy – nor would it pretend to be – the concept of 'circumstance' and 'self' are nevertheless crucial aspects to understanding its content.

While we might ask 'do we write the words, or do the words write us?' [2], the circumstance of our environment, or situation, at the time of speaking – and our individual perspective and interpretation of them – depend equally on one another.

Any attempt to separate these, in a book about how we use language as individuals, would therefore result in the very generalisations we hope to eliminate, and mean that something would be left either incomplete or not done.

* [For these reasons, 'I' – the author – have repeatedly inserted personal comments, with personal perceptions, in an attempt to assist 'you' – the reader – in seeing where this author is coming from and in understanding how the *circumstance* and the *individual* interact, to create situations that inevitably help us to teach language … in context.]

> *'Utterances have meanings in situations.'*
> Geoffrey Leech [3]

These conditions, both tangible and abstract, determine the words we choose to express ourselves.

They include everything and anything that influences our world, our place within it and the power (or lack of) that we have to act within or upon it – how we view ourselves and others, and how it all influences the decisions we make.

We need to know, for example, who the *speaker* is and who they are speaking to – the *hearer*:
- Is the situation urgent, or does it require empathy and tact?
- Is the speaker in need of choosing their words carefully, to avoid risking their reputation?

> All the reference numbers in Part A of *English is Context* are fully explained in the Reference section on page 32.

- Is the subject matter, perhaps, one that can lead to uproar if it isn't handled properly?
- Is the speaker being ironic, or trying to be witty, in order to appear smart or be liked by the hearer?

When we communicate – either as speakers or hearers – we expect to understand, not just the words we use, but the *disguised message* behind them. Traditionally, this seems often to have been overlooked or taken too easily for granted in language teaching.

> **'Assuming the speaker is being co-operative, and not suffering from a brain disorder, we look for the meaning 'between the lines.'**
> Scott Thornbury [4]

This is not always as obvious as it may seem – especially when the language used is not the speaker's or the hearer's first language, or the cultural conditions of the two differ:
- To achieve 'understanding' depends, therefore, not just on knowing the order and individual meaning of words, but also on a competence to recognise how language changes, depending on the context in which it is used.

For two millennia of language teaching, the focus seems very much to have been upon grammar and translation, with a heavy emphasis on learning the alphabet for reading. Within the last hundred years or so, there have been many bold attempts – and excellent proposals and well-founded arguments – for moving away from the grammar-translation method:
- While these may have recognised the need to consider *context*, dealing with it directly, however, seems to remain a grey area in a world known for its many shades of grey.
- While the rules for good conversation are ancient, the study of context is relatively recent and largely theoretical.

This, in my opinion, huge oversight – historically – is comically portrayed in the film *Monty Python's Life of Brian* [5].

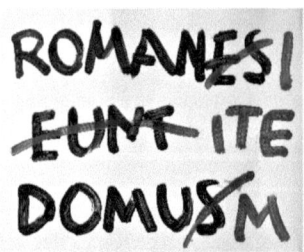

As a new recruit of the *People's Front of Judea* – not to be confused with the *Judean People's Front* – Brian sets out one night on a mission to paint 'Romans go home' on the Forum wall. When he is caught in the act by the sentry on watch, he is reprimanded for his poor grammar and made to write out the correct phrase 100 times across the walls.

Just like teachers who punish their pupils by pointlessly making them write out 'lines', the Roman sentry completely misses the point:
- As an amateur linguist, I enjoy wordplay and puns as much as anyone else, but often with references that are so *obscure* that even my friends are left wondering what on earth I am talking about.
- As an English teacher, while I encourage and praise my learners for being inventive with the language they've learnt, I sympathise when they, as speakers of English as a second or other language, are caught off-guard by people like me – and are faced with the words that they have painstakingly learnt on a course being used in new and unexpected ways.

What can we do to help them?
- A subsequent class discussion, perhaps, or a roleplay?

But other than a not-so-helpful tip – like *'Remember: in English there are always exceptions'* – actual classroom activities have been scarce …

… until now!

See the activity
Any kind of ism ...
on page 106.

Speaking in context

'... you will find that many of the truths that we cling to depend greatly on our point of view.'
Obi-Wan Kenobi, *Return of the Jedi* [6]

There seems to be some disagreement about when we first started talking to one another:
- Some (the 'continuists') believe language evolved slowly from the individual sounds made by our primate ancestors.
- Others (the 'discontinuists') say language is like nothing else to be found in the animal kingdom, and think it must simply have appeared one day, without giving anyone much notice.

In our efforts to dig up the past, we have discovered:

See the activity
DC Onomatopoeia
on page 121.

- a horseshoe-shaped hyoid bone, which supported the tongue of the Neanderthals.
  - This suggests that the species had the capacity to speak.
- a 1,000,000-year-old burial site in caves near Nazareth, Israel.
  - It includes evidence of body ornamentation and tools, and was decorated with painted seashells.
- the oldest-known man-made structure in the world, in a Greek cave first inhabited 135,000 years ago.
  - The 23,000-year-old wall served as a windbreak when things got cold during the ice age.

It is impossible to know *if* or *how well* early species of humans spoke. But, with all of the above in mind, it is difficult to believe that not a word was passed between them – even if it did take them a million years to agree that it was 'a bit nippy outside!'.

Presuming that language did exist so long ago, we can make an educated guess as to what it might have been like.

In 2011, anthropologist Merritt Ruhlen and physicist Murray Gell-Mann carried out extensive research [7] in order to trace the common features of 2,135 languages back to a proto-language spoken in East Africa 50,000 years ago.

The syntax, they discovered, was one of 'subject–object–verb':

See the activity
Classroom tickers
on page 42.

- This means that we can, with some certainty, conclude that a meeting with such early speakers would have been a bit like talking to Yoda (himself a learner/protégé of Obi-Wan Kenobi) from the *Star Wars* stories.

The trouble is that all of this happened long before anybody ever considered who would take the *minutes* of such a meeting.

Writing in context

'To the uneducated an A is just three sticks.'
Winnie-the-Pooh [8]

The idea of writing things down may have started with the Mesopotamians – who also gave us the wheel, mathematics and agriculture:
- Keen to keep track of all this new technology, they began to record their business transactions with a series of notches in clay counters.
- These notches, known as *cuneiform*, represented common goods or features, perhaps in a similar way to how the emblems or faces on coins today represent the denomination.

This icon invites you to stop for a moment as you read, and reflect on what you are reading.

See the activity
Literally figurative
on page 119.

Cuneiform was wholly semantic, could be used in any order and multiples, and – being representations of things rather than words – could be used across large areas between speakers of many different dialects.

The notches evolved: becoming, first, images, then more meaningful units of writing, or graphemes:
- From concrete commodities, they began to represent abstract ideas, then syllables and sounds, and began to be used to record language itself.
- Scribes used the system to note down essays, hymns, poetry and myths, such as the 'Kesh Temple Hymn' [9] and the 'Instructions of Shuruppak' [10].

Written around 2500 BC, these are two of the world's oldest surviving examples of 'literature'.

There is dispute over whether language evolved from imitating sounds or suddenly appeared; and whether *meaning* (semantics) preceded *order* (syntax):
- What do you think is the best way to begin to teach another language?
- What should we start with?
  - Phonetics (the sounds of words);
  - Semantics (words and their meaning as individual units);
  - Syntax (word order).
- What else is important?

For more information on this debate, see Part C: *Ways to think – with the learner in mind* on page 127.

Discourse in context

'When marrying, ask yourself this question: Do you believe that you will be able to converse well with this person into your old age? Everything else in marriage is transitory.'
Friedrich Nietsche [11]

See the activity
An open book
on page 66.

Perhaps the oldest known examples of written discourse were the Sicilian 'mimes' [12].

Written by Sophron of Syracuse in 5000 BC, these mimes were not of the type acted out by silent clowns behind imaginary mirrors, but texts that depicted both the serious and humorous daily events of the Sicilian Greeks.

Plato, who used the dialogues in his own writing, is said to have kept a copy of them under his pillow at night. Despite his efforts to guard them, no copy of these works exists today.

That makes the tablets of the 'Instructions of Shuruppak' mentioned earlier the next contender [13].

Arguably, the first-ever self-help guide, they are believed to have been written by the Sumerian King Shuruppak for his son, Ziusudra, to hold the fort in his absence:
- They include such sage advice as *'by grasping the neck of a huge ox, you can cross the river'.*
- It seems to be undecided if this instruction was meant to be taken metaphorically.

Coincidentally, Shuruppak also includes the first known guidelines for how to *converse*:

- *You should not boast; then your words will be trusted.* (lines 35–38)
  [But don't populist politicians seem to do a lot of the latter?]

- *You should not speak improperly; later it will lay a trap for you.* (42–43)
  [But, as teachers, don't we repeatedly tell our learners that it's important to make mistakes because they will learn from them?]

- *You should not curse strongly; it rebounds on you.* (50)
  [But gentle cursing is OK?]

- *You should not boast in beer halls.* (67)
  [But in wine bars?]

- *You should not pass judgment when you drink beer.* (126)
  [But it's OK when drinking vodka?]

- *You should not speak arrogantly to your mother; that causes hatred for you.* (255–260)
  [But you can say what you like to your father?]

See the activity **Thinking outside the box** on page 45.

It is not known if Ziusudra himself paid any attention or – as might be expected with such paternal advice – sought loopholes in his father's words of wisdom.

Regardless, for the next 2000 years these instructions seemed to suffice.

Change in context

'Evolution normally does not come to a halt, but constantly 'tracks' the changing environment.'
Richard Dawkins [14]

The next notable instructions came in 44 BC, when the Roman philosopher Cicero outlined the rules for good conversation. In *De Officiis* – 'On Duties' – [15], he said that:

- conversation *'should be easy and not in the least dogmatic; it should have the spice of wit'.*
  [I struggle to remember having participated in such civil discourse.]

- the speaker *'should not debar others from participating in it, as if he were entering upon a private monopoly; but, as in other things, so in a general conversation he should think it not unfair for each to have his turn'.*
  [I seem to collect people who do!]

See the activity **Reports are from Mars, rapport is from Venus** on page 89.

- we must be *'on the watch'* and *'shall not betray some defect'* in our character. *'This is most likely to occur, when people in jest or in earnest take delight in making malicious and slanderous statements about the absent, on purpose to injure their reputations.'*
  [Lovely, if that were possible, but – partial to a bit of gossip, as I am – I'm a sceptic.]

- *'it is bad taste also to talk about oneself – especially if what one says is not true'.*
  [Let's not ask my friends how good I am at that!]

While the things we learn from Cicero still apply today, they perhaps refer to *expected* behaviour – with more than just a little wishful thinking:
- They are more useful in identifying the *faults* in discourse than giving *instructions*.

For the Romans, to be courteous it might simply have been enough to differentiate between a '*tu*' – singular, informal 'you' (to use with your close friends) – and '*vos*' – singular, formal 'you' (for those with whom you need to exercise more caution).

This feature – known as the 'T–V distinction' – still exists in the form of very similar words within the different families of Indo-European languages:

- Spanish (Romance) *tú* and *Usted*;
- Dutch (Germanic) *jij* and *U*;
- Russian (Slavic) Tbl (*ty*) and Bbl (*vy*);
- Lithuanian (Baltic) *tu* and *jūs*.

When Germans, for example – who use *du* and *Sie* – get more acquainted with each other, it is not unusual to hear the polite expression *'I would like to offer you a you'*.

In Scots, a West Germanic variety – *thoo* – has fallen out of favour to *ye* ('Hear ye!'), just as 'thou' and 'ye' have given way to *you* in English.

Cicero's language was Latin, and as the German poet Heinrich Heine said: 'if the Romans had been obliged to learn Latin, they would never have found time to conquer the world.' [16]

And indeed, we spent the next two thousand years far more concerned with conquering than with how to conduct our conversations:
- The first 1000 years were ages now popularly referred to as being intellectually 'dark'.
- Then, after that, came a re-birth – or *renaissance* – of enlightenment.

In an attempt to reverse the evolution of language:
- How simple can you make the following sentence?

  I do not know where family doctors acquired illegibly perplexing handwriting; nevertheless extraordinary, pharmaceutical intellectuality counterbalancing indecipherability transcendentalises intercommunication's incomprehensibleness.

See the activity **Circumstantial synonyms** on page 46.

Historically, the English language has been influenced mainly by Germanic (shorter, often mono-syllabic and informal/everyday words) and Romance languages (longer, multisyllabic and formal).

In our sentence, the first word is one letter long, the second is two letters long, the third is three letters long, and so on:
- Can you identify the origin of the words at the beginning and the end of the sentence?

Perhaps not surprisingly, as these words progress (excepting compounds, eg *nevertheless*), their origin changes from Germanic to Latin and Greek – see opposite for more.

The second millennium after Cicero also saw the evolution of the language we call *English*.

English in context

'We have really everything in common with America nowadays except, of course, language.'
Oscar Wilde [17]

Like it or lump it, the language (or languages, depending on your preference) that has (or have) evolved to become what we now call Modern English is/are easily the most widely spoken and written language(s) – ever! The traits that have made it notorious among its estimated 1.1 billion speakers include:
- a *mostly* s-v-o word order;
- an *almost* complete loss of grammatical case;
- the *common* use of an auxiliary 'do';
- a *gradual* regularisation of irregular verbs (eg *dreamed* instead of *dreamt*);
- *you* – a singular and plural second-person personal pronoun, used as both the subject and object … mostly!

A little bit of etymology

I do not know where family doctors acquired illegibly perplexing handwriting; nevertheless extraordinary, pharmaceutical intellectuality counterbalancing indecipherability transcendentalises intercommunication's incomprehensibleness.

One, two, three …

This sentence is popularly shared online – as an example of a sentence where each consecutive word is one letter more than the last:
- The first word is one letter long.
- The second word is two letters long.
- The third word is three letters long …

and so on.

However, it is *also* interesting etymologically.

As the words get longer and have more than one syllable – with the exception of compounds: eg *handwriting* and *nevertheless* – the origin of the words changes: from Anglo-Saxon to Latin and Greek:

☐ This demonstrates that, while common words in everyday English speech are of Germanic origin, the more formal, technical or scientific words have a Latin origin.
☐ This also demonstrates, perhaps, that the French are to blame for 'more sophisticated' (higher level) English vocabulary!

Not only, but also …

It is important to remember that:
☐ Similar words will also appear in other languages which have their origins in Latin and Germanic.
☐ Care should also be taken, however, as although these words have the same origin, they are often not able to be used interchangeably in different languages.
☐ While the English word *doctor* (see opposite) can be used colloquially to describe someone who is qualified to treat people medically, this is not the case with the Spanish word *doctor*.

I	Old English / Germanic
do	Old English / Germanic
not	Middle English / Germanic
know	Old English / Germanic
where	Middle English / Germanic
family	Latin
doctors	Latin
acquired	Middle English / Latin
illegibly	Latin
perplexing	Latin
handwriting	Old English / Germanic
nevertheless	Old English / Germanic
extraordinary	Latin
pharmaceutical	Greek
intellectuality	Latin
counterbalancing	Latin
indecipherability	Latin
transcendentalises	Latin
intercommunication's	Latin
incomprehensibleness	Latin

Simply register at www.deltapublishing.co.uk and search for the ISBN 501742 to download a much fuller description of the etymology of these words, as well as this page.

For the last few hundred years of the last millennium, writers and educators busied themselves with prescribing:
- how English should be spoken and written correctly;
- how we should behave in social contexts: *minding our manners* and *watching our ps & qs*.

… and pouring scorn – and, in some cases, creating a roguish stigma – on in-group attempts to recapture the plural pronoun: *youse, y'all, you 'orrible lot*.

See the activity
English by radio
on page 40.

Although there are arguably many more varieties, Modern English is often sub-divided into three categories: British (BrE), North American (NAE) and Southern Hemisphere:
- Taken out of context, English has the potential of being the language that can have the most *understandings*.
- Similarly, taken out of context, and given its scale, it is potentially also the language that leads to the most *misunderstandings*.

How we converse, rather than how to converse, has subsequently begun to attract the attention of philosophers, linguists, writers … and, inevitably, teachers.

Communication in context

'In fact, 'Ooh, isn't it cold?' – like 'Nice day, isn't it?' and all the others – is English code for 'I'd like to talk to you – will you talk to me?', or, if you like, simply another way of saying 'hello'.'
Kate Fox [18]

See the activity
An elephant in the classroom
on page 112.

Unless we intentionally want there to be a breakdown in communication [I once had a learner who was going to work at the European Commission in Brussels and wanted classes to learn how to be verbose without really *saying* anything!] or simply don't care about the offence we cause to the hearer, we look for ways to be diplomatic.

Fewer misunderstandings arise, according to a study by Juliane House at the University of Hamburg [19], when speakers of different languages use English to communicate with each other than when they communicate with those who use it as a first language.

This suggests that being able to communicate with speakers of English on any *higher* level, and not simply getting the basic message across, it is not sufficient to know the words and their order:
- We also need to be able to analyse and interpret the 'implicature' – or implied meaning – that is not expressed directly.

As Katharina, a learner from Lausanne, Switzerland, remarked: *'Being proficient is when native speakers are not amused or irritated by you!'*

See the activity
Word of the year
on page 48.

When non-native speakers of English, for example, are not familiar with how we manipulate words, or perhaps choose specific words for a situation:
- we may be quick to dismiss those speakers as being rude or thoughtless;
- we may even laugh at their attempts to be understood.

A BBC 80s sitcom set in occupied France, *'Allo 'Allo!*, made fun of how:
- speakers of other languages pronounce English – eg *What-a mistake-a to make-a; zat vas very amuzink*;
- speakers of English fail in the pronunciation of other languages – eg *Good moaning; I am wicking this woo because my polocoman's troosers are full of deenamote*;
- speakers of (British) English sound to speakers of other languages – eg *Toodle pip! Good Show! Bang on! Old fruit!*

… while they were all supposed to be speaking French!

Connotations in context

'Every word has consequences. Every silence, too.'
Jean-Paul Sartre [20]

It is plausible that the French are to blame for how we say (or don't say) things in context:

- When the Norman king, William the Bastard, conquered England in 1066 (and in the process, earned himself a somewhat more heroic name: William the Conqueror) the language of officialdom (politics, law, education, the arts and religion) in England, became heavily influenced by Latin.
- French remained the language of the aristocracy for over three hundred years – which was also the most prolific time for borrowing words from French and having no intention of giving them back.
- A speaker's ability to use these 'formal' words of Latin origin became a sign of intelligence and acceptance by high society, while words of Anglo-Saxon origin remained the language of the people.

Such contrasts in the early development of English, as well as the varying degree of these influences in different regions, meant that native speakers, too, can be equally prone to misunderstandings between one another – especially if communicating with speakers from other, very different, contexts or backgrounds:

- For example: between a Ugandan hotel receptionist and an Irish tourist, a Bahamian minister, a Hong Kong bank manager or a Fijian carpenter.

'English' perhaps began to come into its own right during the reign of Henry IV (1367–1413), the first monarch of England to speak English as his first language:

- '… *all are banished till their conversations appear more wise and modest to the world*', declared Prince John in Shakespeare's play, *Henry IV Part 2* [21], believed to have been written between 1596 and 1599.

Within fifty years of that play, Prince John's warning was put to the test. The foolish actions of the king of a united England, Scotland and Ireland – Charles I – meant that he was not only banished but it also lost him his head.

These are the words of John O'Farrell in the intriguingly titled *An Utterly Impartial History of Britain or 2000 years of Upper Class Idiots in Charge* [22] – a light-hearted poke at some pretty foolish monarchs and the consequences of their actions:

- *'Charles 1 (1625–49) combined all the arrogance and certainty of the English upper classes with an acute lack of intelligence and a natural tendency to deceive … he stammered and argued furiously with his wife over such matters as whether or not it was raining.'*

Charles' reign ended in a civil war:

- The people divided.
- The previously united kingdoms became one republic.

Ten years later, Charles II reclaimed the throne. His father's lesson learnt, the new king was definitely up for the idea of talking to people – and with the revolutionary notion of including women!

Conversation in context

'Conversation has been described as an art, as a game, sometimes even as a battle. … The analysis of conversation turns out to be one of the most fascinating in linguistic study for that very reason.'
David Crystal [23]

See the activity
A taboo U-turn
on page 122.

See the activity
The Shakespeare hop
on page 92.

See the activity
A guided tour of the news
on page 101.

'Conversation' salons were set up to provide the aristocracy with not only somewhere to play cards and dance, but a place to discuss the important topics of the day – such as literature and the arts.

Europe at this time remained a hotbed of revolution. This meant that topics like religion and politics either had to be avoided, or 'wise and modest' (Prince John again [24]) ways had to be found to deal with them:

- Metaphor, implied meaning, idiom – and an understatement that came to be recognised as characteristically 'British' – had to be used to keep one's head on one's shoulders.

See the activity
Taboo in role
on page 43.

- Foes could no longer be sure if what was *said* was what was *meant*.

In Britain, in the centuries that followed, there were no more civil wars, revolutions or republics. A person's conversation became a measure of their worth – good education and wit reflected their standing in society:

- Writers used discourse as a valuable tool to bring their characters to life, encouraging readers to assess their respectability, trustworthiness and intent.

This, and the behaviour that accompanied it, became generally known as *polite*:

- '… *from Latin politus "refined, elegant, accomplished". Used literally at first in English; sense of "elegant, cultured" is first recorded c.1500, that of "behaving courteously" is 1748.*' [25]

The analysis of politeness (not to be confused with linguistic politeness – see 'Politeness in context' on page 21) – remains a feature of today's exams in formal education.

As English grew rich in vocabulary, with borrowings from the languages of an ever expanding empire, it also became known for its implied meaning, indirectness and tact – a language you could 'play' with.

Illustrators of seaside postcards, cartoonists – and now designers of internet memes – have all poked fun at its ambiguity, double meaning and innuendo – a code that seemed to make sense only to its speakers.

Conversationalists in context

'"What ho!" I said.
"What ho!" said Motty.
"What ho! What ho!"
"What ho! What ho! What ho!"
After that it seemed rather difficult to go on with the conversation.'
P G Wodehouse, *My Man Jeeves* [26]

Discourse in English, just like in other languages, is like a ball game of tackles, passes and deliveries.

To convince others of their ability, learners of English are often expected to:
- understand the implied meaning;
- recognise the social connotations of the language we use;
- know how we manipulate language to our advantage, according to the context in which it is used.

See the activity
Dinner date from history
on page 44.

How successful they are depends wholly on the players.

In the 1930s, a now obscure (and outdated) author, Milton Wright, attempted to classify conversationalists beyond their age, sex and superiority, in his book about good conversation, *The Art of Conversation* [27].

Among the 'offenders against good conversation', Wright listed:
☐ *the annoying interrupter*
☐ *the mental absentee*
☐ *the belittler*
☐ *the gusher*
☐ *the habitual grouch*
☐ *the ubiquitous windbag*
☐ *the frivolous wisecracker*
☐ *the confirmed preacher*
☐ *the glorified self*
☐ *the ready debater*
☐ *slovenly slangsters –*   *careless, unthinking talkers*
☐ *the intolerant*
☐ *gossips*
☐ *the man who wants something*
☐ *risqué raconteurs*
☐ *the microscopist*
☐ *the cross-examiner*
☐ *the single-tracker –*   *'harping on one string'*
☐ *the die-hard –*   *'he won't give in'*
☐ *the too serious –*   *and 'direct antithesis of the habitual wisecracker'*

See the activity
Dinner date from history
on page 44.

See the activity
It takes one to know one
on page 96.

In contrast, among some desirable qualities, he listed:
☐ *Speakers should keep in tune.*
☐ *Possess a sense of the dramatic.*
☐ *Be moderate.*
☐ *Always be in good humour.*
☐ *Be neither a yes nor a no man.*
☐ *Show charity and unselfishness.*
☐ *Keep their minds flexible*

But just as we were getting to grips with conversation, we went back to more conquering.

The world went to war and *The Art of Conversation* made an unnoticed exit from the shelves of popular reading.

Codes in context

"'Why do they call you the Duck?"
"Because it rhymes with 'luck'. See, my daddy always told me to be just like a duck. Stay smooth on the surface and paddle like the devil underneath."'
Martin 'Rubber Duck' Penwald, *Convoy* [28]

The wars of the twentieth century, including two world wars, meant that this became a time for finding novel ways to elude enemies with secret messages. Besides using complex encryption machines, such as Enigma, it was soon realised that the enemies were – coincidentally – speakers of other languages, and that 'in-group exclusive' varieties of language could be equally impenetrable:

- The English actor Wilfred Pickles was enlisted to broadcast news across the North Sea in Yorkshire English.
- Native Americans used their own languages (such as Cherokee, Choctaw and Navajo) to transmit their manoeuvres. They became known as the 'code-talkers'.

See the activity **Mincing your words** on page 107.

Thinkers, known as *linguists* (not a reflection of how many languages they were able to speak, but of how language is spoken), became interested in, and began to study, the codes that had been established within the languages that we speak.

Often, these had developed, over many generations, as non-standard *patois* (dialects of low regard) or *pidgin* (a word, which, curiously, is believed to originate from a mispronunciation of 'business'):

- They were intended to either facilitate communication when trading, or to intentionally mislead or deceive authority. Examples of the latter include:
- Rhyming slang – such as Australian, Cockney, or Glasgow – used seemingly nonsensical terms such as *barnet* (Barnet Fair – hair); *having something half-inched* (pinched) or *going for an Andy Murray* (curry). We are not sure who is to be credited for such inventive and playful speech: market traders, the criminal underworld, migrant communities – or, conversely, locals wary of outsiders?

See the activity **Have you Meghan Markled?** on page 43.

- Polari – once popular among, but not exclusive to, actors and those considered to be outcasts of society. Where homosexuality was regarded a serious crime, for example, Polari was adopted simply as a way to survive.

In these examples of what Michael Halliday [29] called *anti-language*, the speaker's hope may originally have been to dupe or exclude those who did not 'belong'. But rather than being *secret* codes, they created a camaraderie, a sense of community – of being 'in this together'.

Perhaps, in a similar way, internet gamers have created new terms that, although shared with others around the world, will baffle the teacher if used in the classroom:

- Or in the same way that news channels such as the Senegalese *Journal Rappé* have discovered an increasingly popular way to 'reach the people' – by rapping the news!

Though the 'anti-language' may eventually die out, some examples make it into present-day speech:
- Which of the below do you use/would you teach?
  - Polari: *barney* (n.), *bevvy* (n.), *manky* (adj.), *naff* (adj.), *scarper* (vb.), *palaver* (n.)
  - Rhyming slang: *use your loaf, take the mickey, tell porkies, have a butcher's*
  - Gamer slang: *ditch* (vb.), *co-op* (vb.), *boss* (n.), *noob* (n.)

Speech in context

'It was for too long the assumption of philosophers that the business of a 'statement' can only be to 'describe' some state of affairs, or to 'state some fact', which it must do either truly or falsely.'
John Longshaw Austin [30]

At first sight, and without much forethought, words may seem simple enough in their meaning, but the twentieth century was a turning point in understanding how they perform. Philosophers began to question the difference between the literal meaning of the words that we use – and what they *suggest* or *insinuate*:

- Ludwig Wittgenstein (1889–1951) told us, in his Philosophical Investigations, 'the meaning of a word is its use in the language' and called the 'actions into which it is woven, the 'language-game'. [31]
- John Longshaw Austin (1911–1960) in a lecture at Harvard University – 'How to do things with words' – proposed the idea that the things we say perform a function and do things. [32]

This led to the Theory of Speech Acts.

In the words of Austin:
'Going back into the history of a word, very often into Latin, we come back pretty commonly to pictures or models of how things happen or are done. These models may be fairly sophisticated and recent, as is perhaps the case with 'motive' or 'impulse', but one of the commonest and most primitive types of model is one which is apt to baffle us through its very naturalness and simplicity.' [33]

> See the activity **You are (not) cordially invited ...** on page 105.

Confusion in context

'If the English language made any sense, 'lackadaisical' would have something to do with a shortage of flowers.'
Doug Larson [34]

Unless you are a member of an indigenous tribe that has had no contact with 21st-century society, for example, it is highly unlikely that you have had *no* contact with English:

- Anyone else, who claims to know nothing of the language, will most likely be familiar with one or more of the following:
  – '*hello*' – as a greeting;
  – '*happy birthday*' – as a way to congratulate someone on the anniversary of their birth;
  – '*please*' – to invite;
  – '*thank you*' – to show gratitude.

> See the activity **Windy lifts, schody stairs** on page 56.

Yet, these same words can baffle us:

- With a slight, if any, change in intonation, these statements can be used to do very different things:
  – '*hello*' as a warning (for someone not to patronise you);
  – '*happy birthday*' as a complaint that, while all might be well with others, it is certainly not so with you;
  – '*please*' (often becoming a disyllabic *per-lease*) as an order to someone to not do something; or as a refusal;
  – '*thank you*' as disagreement or declining to accept or do something.

> See the activity **Afflicted with sarcasm** on page 45.

Greetings, congratulations, invitations, promises, orders and warnings – these are also all examples of how we do things with words:

- *'I'm tired'*, for example, might simply be an assertation of how you feel, but it could equally be a way to:
  - excuse yourself, retire after a long day;
  - excuse yourself for not being able to concentrate or do something as well as you normally might;
  - complain that you've had enough of something (eg *I'm tired of your complaining*).

To competent users of the language, their implied meanings may well seem obvious.

But for words to perform effectively, the *conditions* must be right. If they are not – if the utterance is made, for example, by an actor, or insincerely – the act fails:
- *'Sorry'* is only an apology if the speaker is genuinely apologetic.
- If it is obvious that the speaker is not at all sorry – and perhaps being sarcastic – the hearer doesn't have to think hard about this, it is immediately obvious: because the conditions, known as 'felicity' or 'felicitous', are not right.

See the activity **Felicitous conditions** on page 61.

It is often assumed that unless we are acting, lying, joking or being sarcastic, we want our conversational partners to understand – and cooperate.

Cooperation in context

'"When I use a word," Humpty Dumpty said, in rather a scornful tone, "it means just what I choose it to mean – neither more nor less." "The question is," said Alice, "whether you can make words mean so many different things." "The question is," said Humpty Dumpty, "which is to be master – that's all."'
Lewis Carroll [35]

When we imply something to others, either with non-linguistic features or within the context in which we say it, how successfully we can do this depends on the words we choose at the time of speaking:
- In other words, the success of indirect communication depends on the clues available, and an expectation that, as the speakers, we are being cooperative.

So reasoned Herbert Paul Grice (1913–1988): *'Make your contribution such as it is required, at the stage at which it occurs, by the accepted purpose or direction of the talk exchange in which you are engaged.'* [36]

This *Cooperative Principle*, known popularly as *Grice*, listed four such expectations in its Maxims:
- Manner – avoid obscurity and ambiguity, be brief and orderly.
- Quality – do not say what we believe to be false or lack sufficient evidence.
- Quantity – provide an appropriate level of information: not too little, not too much.
- Relation – be relevant.

See the activity **Only half the story!** on page 52.

Grice's maxims were not intended to be a set of conversational instructions – such as those set in stone by King Shuruppak all those years ago – but, instead, an early attempt to help us understand how we say things indirectly.

Imagine visiting another town and looking for a place to eat. You read that the local pub, *The Coach and Horses*, served a good lunch. You stop a stranger to ask the way.

According to Grice, you would naturally assume that person will be helpful and give you the clear and direct instructions that you need to find your way:
- If they accidentally gave you the instructions to another pub, *The Wagon and Horses*, they would be 'violating' Grice's maxims and probably be very apologetic once they realised their mistake.

- If, on the other hand, the stranger asked why on earth you would want to go there, and told you about the other pubs which were much nearer, you would probably understand that the stranger didn't want you to go there, without directly saying so. This would be what Grice termed 'flouting' the maxims of the Cooperative Principle.

See the activity **Song lyrics roleplays** on page 57.

Consider how the following lyrics from popular English songs flout Grice's maxims:
– 'We are the world, we are the children, we are the ones who make a brighter day, so let's start giving.'
– 'And you're here in my heart. And my heart will go on and on.'
– 'Confusion in her eyes that says it all. She's lost control.'
– 'And everybody knows that the Plague is coming, everybody knows that it's moving fast.'
– 'Everybody's heard about the bird, bird, bird, bird, b-bird's the word.'

- Can these be translated directly?
- Would they work in another language?

See the activity **Donald, Where's Your Troosers?** on page 81.

When an American President says *Make America great again*, the success of this phrase depends on the audience's expectation that the speaker is being cooperative:
- In this case, the meaning – or what Grice called the 'conversational implicature' – of the word *great*:
  – depends on the audience believing that there is already something very wrong with the nation.
  – implies that, by following the speaker, there will be a change for what – he believes – is the better.

The President expects that – by avoiding any explanation of how greatness can be achieved or what it means, but by appealing to listeners who are members of a larger, disenchanted 'group' – they will come to the conclusion that 'he says what everybody is thinking'.

Grice set a cat among the pigeons.

As soon as the Cooperative Principle was published, linguists began throwing their arms up in the air:
- They argued that the idea was 'culturally specific'.
- In other cultures and contexts, *being cooperative* depended on different principles, such as the speaker being taken literally, sincerely – and at face value.

Perhaps they had a point – in an age where 'post truths' and 'conspiracy theories' are everyday terms, how concerned are we about committing to certainty?

To explain how different cultures and their languages interact indirectly, Geoffrey Leech (1936–2014) proposed a principle of his own.

He called it the *Politeness Principle*.

Politeness in context

'People are not just in the business of downloading information into each other's heads but are social animals concerned with the impressions they make.'
Steven Pinker [37]

The things we say can not only perform a function within the context that they are used, they also have the power to influence, motivate, persuade, endear, upset, enrage, please, satisfy, cheer, and confuse.

Where Grice was interested in how things can be said *indirectly*, Leech was concerned with the *impressions* that our utterances have upon the hearer(s). This has become generally known as 'linguistic politeness' and should not be confused with *courtesy*. (See 'Conversation in context' on page 14.)

Leech's politeness maxims were:

See the activity
Avoidance charades
on page 114.

- Tact – speaking in terms of the benefit to the hearer.
  - For example: Leech compared the phrase 'Peel these potatoes' with 'Do have another sandwich'.
  While both sentences are orders, the second is much 'friendlier' – or more polite – as it offers a positive reward for doing whatever it is and making it difficult for the hearer to refuse.

- Generosity – minimising the benefit to the speaker.
  - For example: comparing 'You must come and have dinner with us' and 'We must come and have dinner with you'.
  And 'Could I borrow your car?' seems kinder and less presumptuous than 'Could you lend me your car?'

See the activity
Flattery will get you …
on page 90.

- Approbation – praising the hearer instead of the speaker.
  - For example: 'How clever of you' and not 'How clever of me'.

- Modesty – minimising the praise of the speaker.
  - For example: 'How stupid of me' is much more clement than 'How stupid of you', which could be seen as a personal attack.

See the activity
The Spaghetti Challenge
on page 104.

- Agreement – seeking to avoid disagreement between the speakers.
  - For example: saying 'That's interesting' instead of voicing your disapproval.
  'I hear what you say …' respects the hearer's opinion, even though everyone knows there is a 'but' coming.

- Sympathy – expressing feeling and understanding with the hearer.
  - For example: 'I'm so sorry to hear your team lost the game' will endear the speaker to the hearer more than 'I'm so pleased to hear your team lost the game'.

While the non-preferred sentences above may seem unlikely, they are often adopted in a playful way, or by those who purposefully attempt to inflame or attack group members.

See the activity
Trollhunters
on page 72.

In gaming forums and social media platforms, people who do this are known as 'trolls'.

Apply the Politeness Principle to the following sentences by continuing them or giving them a context so that they sound natural or friendly:
- *Wash my car …*
- *We must visit your office …*
- *You're crazy …*
- *That's just wrong …*
- *I'm so pleased you didn't get the job …*

In contrast to Grice, Leech's politeness maxims *were* culturally dependent – in other words, the effect of what we say, and how we say it, depends on what is considered appropriate in a particular *culture*.

Knowing how to show respect and consideration towards others helps us avoid humiliation or embarrassment and preserve dignity.

Connections in context

'Vodka – connecting people'
Popular T-shirt/hoodie

Speaking another language, as some might tell you through the bottom of a glass, becomes so much easier after drinking alcohol:
- It removes our inhibitions, and we become less afraid of making fools of ourselves.
- While this is hardly sage advice, it is true that we are all concerned by how others see us, and the impressions we make.

In the Politeness Principle, Leech [38] considered the goal of our interactions, rather than the *implication* of what is said.

To be able to reach that *goal*, we try to gather as much information about the person we communicate with. When making phatic speech, or small talk, for example:
- We ask questions to help us make decisions about character:
  - Do we like this person?
  - Can this person be trusted?

  And we watch for clues that reveal personality:
  - Does this person talk excessively about himself/herself?

- We try to find things in common, and we use the language that we hope will be most effective to connect.
- We pay careful attention to the background of the speakers (race, age, sex, social standing, etc) and we choose our words, or even adapt our register, carefully to be appropriate for the context.

How we do this, and the subjects we choose to talk about, will also vary between cultures.

So, on each new encounter, we test the water – to see what is safe – and watch for linguistic clues, such as intonation and discourse markers – to gage the enthusiasm (or lack of) of the response.

But don't be surprised if some cultures see through this ploy.

Northern Europeans, for example, are notorious for being direct and to the point:
- Contrary to popular opinion, however, they are not innately rude – they just consider such discourse as pointless, or even insincere.

In an English-speaking context:
- Many English speakers assume a closeness with those they speak to and use terms of endearment, such as 'mate' and 'darling' – much to the bewilderment of speakers of other languages.
- These speakers might also prefer an indirect approach – English, after all, has a wealth of phrases for this, and which depend on an in-group understanding.

It is perhaps not surprising, then, that English native speakers of English have recently received criticism for being poor or exceedingly verbose communicators – in a world where their language is increasingly becoming the global lingua franca for business.

Psychologist Erving Goffman referred to the impression we try to make to connect as our 'face':

'The term face *may be defined as the positive social value a person effectively claims for himself by the line others assume he has taken during a particular contact.'* [39]

See the activity
Claiming common ground
on page 79

See the activity
Clearing the dead wood
on page 75.

See the activity
A royal bastard
on page 80.

Face in context

'I don't care what you think about me, I don't think about you at all.'
Coco Chanel [40]

The choices we make when trying to make an impression (good, bad or shocking) depend on our cultural and linguistic backgrounds. Those of us who communicate with members of different cultures – such as language teachers when meeting new learners, for example – must make careful choices each time we enter into communication.

Ask yourself some questions:
- How would you like your learners to see you?
- How do you connect and gain their trust?
- How well do you know the lesson topic?
- Do you worry you might bore the class with it?

The respect your learners hold for you will depend on your answers to these questions.

When you walk into your class, you will not just have planned your 'lesson':
- You may also have made conscious decisions about …
    - the clothes you wear;
    - your general appearance;
    - your approach to your teaching;
    - how you will interact with your learners.

As you teach, you will choose the words that you use carefully, adapting your language according to the learners' level – to make sure you are understood:
- If your learners are a group of teenagers, or have a common speciality, you might risk throwing in some jargon or slang in an attempt to gain their respect. If you are out of your depth, though, this could also have the opposite effect.
- If your learner is a top executive, the context might be more formal. You might have some jokes up your sleeve, but the appropriacy of these depends heavily on the right context and culture.

We can potentially *lose* face with the very first words we utter.

See the activity
Age, sex, location?
on page 84.

To prevent this from happening, we adopt strategies of politeness to make sure that we make a positive impression (meet our 'face needs').

These strategies provide us with an escape route:
- Should things not go to plan, they will allow us to 'hedge' the things we say and plead innocence, blaming any negativity on a simple misunderstanding.

Face is determined not just by the people but also by the social surroundings in which we find ourselves, which we might collectively call 'context'.

In context, politeness helps us to protect ourselves – from ourselves.

Face threats in context

'Where wolf's ears are, wolf's teeth are near.'
The Saga of the Völsungs [41]

In *Politeness: Universals in Language Usage*, Penelope Brown and Stephen Levinson [42] provided an inventory of strategies to help us avoid potential threats to our positive face.

They called these threats 'Face Threatening Acts (FTAs)'.

The strategies to minimise them were:

- 'Bald on record' – saying things directly, and doing nothing to minimise a threat to the speaker's face:
  - It avoids confusion and ambiguity, and can be effective in getting a message across urgently, but lacks tact and, in less urgent cases, is often seen as an affront.

- 'Positive politeness' – a need to be accepted and liked by others. By sharing attitudes and values, and by claiming empathy and friendship with the person we are speaking to, we recognise their desire for respect and a need to be appreciated:
  - It includes speaking in terms of a team – 'we are in this boat together' – joking, paying compliments, exaggerating interest and using terms of endearment. But too much of this, and you could come across as either overbearing or insincere.

- 'Negative politeness' – this is more oriented to maintaining a distance between the speakers, and assumes that, by asking for something, we are imposing upon that person:
  - It includes apologising for the intrusion, being pessimistic about the outcome (*I don't suppose you could …*), hedging or fuzzy language (*Would you, Could you …?*) and using honorifics (*Sir/Madam*, etc).

- 'Off record' – using hints and suggestions that depend on the hearer's ability to guess what the speaker wants:
  - While it is perhaps tactful, its ambiguity often leads to misunderstanding.

It is important to mention here that, when speaking about politeness strategies, the terms 'positive' and 'negative' are neutral: *'They're just different, like electric currents can be termed positive or negative without being better or worse than one another'* – in the words of author and teacher trainer Vicki Hollett [43].

> See the activity ***How are you polite?*** on page 36.

> See the activity ***Reasons to steer clear*** on page 113.

Imagine that you are trying to assimilate into a new culture, as my family was in South-West Scotland, and you are in a busy café:

- You have ordered breakfast and want to sit, but all the tables are occupied.
- You see one table where a very well-dressed, elderly man is seated alone reading a broadsheet newspaper. It is spread across the table in front of him.
- You consider an approach.

Which politeness strategy will you use?

- *'Move aside!'*
  - Is it your right as a customer to sit here?

- *'Can I join you here, mate?'*
  - Will he like you if you call him 'mate'?

- *'I don't suppose there's room for one more here?'*
  - Should he say no, that is fine: you have already said that you didn't suppose there was room.

- *'Popular place, this!'*
  - Will he understand what you want, and offer you a place?

- *Avoid approaching the person altogether.*
  - Surely, once he realises the café is full, he will make room.

We can list a number of factors that will influence our choice of words. For example:

- You (the speaker)/the person at the table (the hearer):
  - gender/age/attire/expression/mood/smell;
- The context:
  - the time of day; whether you both speak the same language; level of noise (eg next to a speaker/TV set); people at other tables who look like they may be leaving soon.

All of these factors have the potential to create a threat to our – metaphorical – face.

Face saving in context

'Why is face so important? Face represents one's self-esteem, reputation, status, and dignity. Face is social currency.'
Maya Hu-Chan [44]

The English language is full of popular phrases – such as metaphors and idioms – whose success depends on 'face saving' strategies such as the above.

Consider the following examples:

- *'Humour me!'* – (negative politeness): you realise that what you are saying or asking of the listener is patronising or already obvious.
  - By using this phrase, you are explaining that there is a reason to the madness and subsequently saving face.
- *'That's a brave proposal.'* – (off record): the speaker may be suggesting that the hearer's proposal is either ridiculous or unlikely – if the hearer is the speaker's employer, for example, perhaps diplomacy is necessary.
  - However, the use of *brave* may also be interpreted as being courageous and noble, and that the speaker supports the idea.
- *'I'm not a racist/sexist but …'* – (negative politeness): the speaker knows that what he/she is about to say may be controversial, and attempts to excuse the saying of it, but nevertheless feels the need to do so.
  - It is unlikely to work, as the severity of the comment will probably cancel what was said before.
- *'S/he's had a chequered past.'* – (positive politeness): an idiom that means that someone has had a disreputable past.
  - By using such idioms, we avoid having to say more or give a detailed history. Though there may be alternatives in other languages, they are not always translatable.
- *'Nudge nudge; wink wink; say no more.'* – (off record): a line from a sketch by the British comedy team Monty Python, emphasised to hilarious effect.
  - These are a series of indirect and obscure statements that are nevertheless understood completely by the hearer.

These phrases are culturally specific, and rely heavily upon a strong understanding of English in context – learners of English as a second language will not only struggle to translate them to their first language but, even if they are successful, the *speech act* will be lost.

It is important, therefore, not just to understand the *words* but to understand how they *behave* in the context in which they are used:

- Learners who are able to overcome this comprehension hurdle, and can use such phrases

See the activity
Brutally civil
on page 118.

See the activity
Mark my words
on page 116.

appropriately, have reached pragmatic competence.
- They have every reason to be proud of themselves – and their smile of satisfaction, will probably be all too evident!

We have spoken, so far, of maintaining a favourable image of ourselves by being cooperative and polite in our discourse.

See the activity
The heckle therapist
on page 93.

We should not ignore, however, that there are times when we are confronted by those who certainly do not care about the impression they make, have no intention of being liked and are definitely *not* cooperative!

Impoliteness in context

'That's a repressive society where you can't be horrible, I'm not horrible, they made me horrible, I'm just honest.'
John Lydon (aka Johnny Rotten) [45]

Impoliteness in English-speaking cultures is possibly much more prevalent than we may like to think:
- But it does not follow that native speakers are an angry bunch of so and sos.

It is perhaps for the very reason that we use so many politeness strategies that *flouting* these expectations will do all of the following:
- not only provide shock and outrage in the arts (eg punk rock, street art);
- but also feed comedy (eg Ricky Gervais, South Park, etc);
- and even find a place in family entertainment (such as *The Weakest Link* game show).

See the activity
Mind your Ps and Qs!
on page 44.

Similarly, being *overly* polite can have the opposite effect.

In an attempt to recognise what constitutes impoliteness, Jonathan Culpeper mirrored Brown and Levinson to provide what he called a 'taxonomy of impoliteness strategies' [46].

Consider the earlier example of a crowded café:
- It could be that the seated gentleman in question clearly sees you standing in the hope of being seen and noticed but, for whatever reason, he chooses to ignore you.

The situation is no longer amicable.

You now have a number of options:

- Bald on-record impoliteness:
  - You say something directly and unambiguously to the man.
  - You express exactly what you think of his lack of compassion for you not having somewhere to sit.

- Positive impoliteness:
  - You no longer care about being liked.
  - You use offensive identity markers, make fun of or abuse the man.
  - You might even use profanity to point out what you think of him.
  - You show no regard for his right to privacy.

- Negative impoliteness:
  - You do not care about any imposition you might make.
  - You threaten or attempt to frighten the man, pour scorn over his behaviour or are otherwise contemptuous.

- Off-record impoliteness:
  - You avoid direct impoliteness – with sarcasm, for example, to show how you feel.

- You thank him for so kindly moving, even if he clearly has no intention of doing so.
- You make other indirect comments – in an attempt to shame him.

Or, in the interest of good 'education'/manners, you might choose to say nothing – but also refrain from any further politeness.

Sadly, many language teachers will shy away from the language of conflict – perhaps in a shared/common understanding that we should not directly teach or encourage our learners how to be impolite:
- Being on the receiving end of such behaviour, especially in a second language, perhaps requires greater survival skills than any other situation.

But, as mentioned earlier, it is important to remember that impoliteness can be deceptive:
- What may be taboo in some English-speaking cultures, will be toyed with in others.

Profanity, insults and inappropriate identity markers can be the essence of banter – acceptable, even expected, ways to express intimacy between friends and groups – while other 'receivers' will be confused, or even offended.

Such 'mock impoliteness', therefore, becomes a feature of 'positive politeness' – but it will only be successful if this is commonly understood, and the context is relevant.

Relevance in context

'There are no dirty words, only dirty minds.'
Lenny Bruce [47]

Despite the stacks of holiday phrasebooks on offer at airport bookshops, our everyday interactions are not quite as simple as putting our thoughts or intentions into an appropriate code, for the hearer to understand exactly what we want to express.

Instead, each and every word that we use, as Dan Sperber and Derdrie Wilson proposed in their work on 'relevance' in 1986 [48], carries a connotation that will be understood *individually* – according to the context in which it is used.

Consider, for example, a teacher at the start of a new term who asks his/her learners how they spent their holidays:
- When they reply that they did 'nothing', they probably do not mean that they were cryogenically frozen until it was time to come back to school.
- While they would be much more explicit in a courtroom, within the context of the classroom it is generally understood that what they did do is too uninteresting, or none of anybody else's business, to mention – and, subsequently, *irrelevant*.

Relevance Theory proposes the following steps in transmitting a message:
- The hearer follows a 'path of least effort' to arrive at what he/she believes to be most appropriate within the context in which it is said.
- Once reaching that assumption, he/she stops trying to interpret any further.

You might argue that this is not the case when reading song lyrics, poetry, etc, but agree that it is probably true of conversation.

But even then, how often have we wanted to do an oral double-take – to discover if what the speaker *said* was actually what we first *understood*?

A T-shirt spotted in Eastern Europe brandishes a picture of the Russian revolutionary Vladimir Lenin. Next to him are his famous words *'Learn, learn, learn'*. On the reverse of the T-shirt, however, are the words *'… from the past'*.

See the activity
Pick 'n' mix
on page 41.

See the activity
Roger Irrelevant
on page 58.

See the activity
Larkin' about
on page 59.

See the activity **Blame it on the boogie** on page 53.

The simple message is open to at least two interpretations, depending on the mindset of the reader:
- If the reader believes that the Soviet occupation of Eastern Europe was an atrocity which must never be allowed to be repeated, the message received by the reader will be to never let such a thing happen again.
- If, on the other hand, the reader is a strong believer in the Soviet ideal, he/she may interpret the message as 'learn from the mistakes we made' so that the next time around things will last.

Once the reader reaches one of these interpretations, it may become difficult for them to change their understanding of the message.

In 2020, civil rights protests broke out in many countries, notably the US, UK and Canada, headed by an organisation whose motto was *Black Lives Matter*:
- To – hopefully – most of us, this message was clearly an expression to recognise the massive loss of lives as a result of slavery, institutionalised racism (eg in the police forces), discrimination and white supremacy.
- But a more paranoid mind might take offence at the slogan, understanding the message as '*Black lives matter – ours don't*'.

Perhaps a better slogan would be *All Lives Matter*:
- But would this be missing the point?

See the activity **Greta's world** on page 73.

How language works within one culture, society or group will not necessarily apply in another.

And all of this is, of course, very individual:
- Many have read some of the world's greatest books, made their decisions – and remain adamant about what the author meant.

Knowing what is appropriate or relevant in situations, therefore, depends on our level of 'pragmatic competence'.

So far, we have seen how language, in particular English, has developed, and how *context* influences its use. The study of this use in context is known among linguistic scholars as *pragmatics*. We will now see how introducing pragmatics to our classrooms can help our learners finally understand not just what we *say*, but also what we really *mean*.

Pragmatics in context

'By giving our students practice in talking with others, we give them frames for thinking on their own.'
Lev S. Vygotsky [49]

See the activity
I see black for you
on page 68.

The recognition, and subsequent study, of how words take on different meanings, depending on the context, is known as 'pragmatics'.

To understand how we communicate, and the conventions for discourse, it is helpful to consider its historical background.

It has its origins in Speech Act Theory and developed from Goffman's observations of our attempts or wants to save face [50], the Cooperative (Grice) and Politeness (Leech) Principles, and how others have explored these theories.

Brown and Levinson's work on politeness [51], according to Dr. Jonathan Culpeper, professor and author:

'… is still the most important model we have – the most comprehensive and the most tested. Of course, what people have been doing is trying to devise something to replace it, but they haven't got there yet.' [52]

The strategies of politeness can provide a useful key to understanding how speakers of different languages express and imply what they want, and how they are understood by others.

Teaching pragmatics in context

'We cannot create observers by saying 'observe' but by giving them the power and the means for this observation, and these means are procured through education of the senses.'
Maria Montessori [53]

Pragmatics is to structured language instruction what driving lessons are to a theory test: it puts the theory into practice:
- One without the other might make it possible to 'muddle through' but, to achieve maximum control, it is important to have a good balance of both.

Historically, language learning seems to have been a victim of solely extrinsic instruction, measuring a learner's ability to provide a given answer – regardless of the context:
- With a focus almost exclusively on syntax and semantics, there has been little room for manoeuvre in a subject as adaptable as language.

See the activity
Literally speaking
on page 74.

To exaggerate the failings of such a rigid programme, you have only to google 'smart-ass kids answers to test questions' to find examples such as:
- Question: *What ended in 1945?*
  Answer: *1944.*
- Question: *Can you motivate your answer?*
  Answer: *Go, answer, go!*

The sheer cheek of such answers will – depending on your point of view – either be annoying or hilarious and, in all likelihood, will have a big red cross or 'wrong' written next to it by the teacher:
- While we do not condone such responses, is it right to punish such thinking?

See the activity
Thinking outside the box on page 45.

What happens here could be a breakdown in communication – if the learner is particularly obtuse – or a 'smart-ass' attempt to outsmart the teacher.

Learning pragmatics in context

'That is what learning is. You suddenly understand something you've understood all your life, but in a new way.'
Doris Lessing [54]

Both situations above could perhaps be compared to the predicaments faced by language learners who, after spending years studying a second language, discover a huge gap between what they *thought* they knew from the classroom and their ability to *communicate* effectively.

One such learner (we'll call him Gintas) recalled:
- how, for many years, he had collected comics, instruction booklets, historical texts – any printed material that he could lay his hands on that might help him to learn;
- how he had painstakingly translated them all – until he acquired an excellent knowledge of vocabulary and sentence structure.
- how, for all of that time, he had no-one to interact with in the language he was trying to learn.

When the opportunity finally arose, despite all his learning, he was barely able to communicate.

See the activity
Soap bubbles
on page 62.

To demonstrate quite simply how many coursebook dialogues fail to reflect real-life situations, Kathleen Bardovi-Harlig, in her study *Pragmatics and Language Teaching: Bringing Pragmatics and Pedagogy Together* [55], recommends that we consider how unnaturally these dialogues end:
- *'Have two students read the dialogue, then walk away from each other when they reach the end. The effect is immediate and obvious.'*

This difference between the language that we use in given situations – 'competence' – and what we are able do with it – 'performance' – was also recognised by Chomsky [56]:
- *'Linguistic theory is concerned with an ideal speaker-listener in a completely homogeneous speech community, who knows its language perfectly and is unaffected by such grammatically irrelevant conditions as memory limitations, distractions, shifts of attention and interest, and errors (random or characteristic) in applying his knowledge of the language in actual performance.'*

Teaching pragmatics in English

'Education is not the filling of a pail, but the lighting of a fire.'
Variously attributed to Socrates, Plutarch and W. B. Yeats [57]

More recently, we have made a conscious effort to include more 'performance-based' activities in our English classes.

See the activity
Comic strip(tease)
on page 97.

Considering context will, for example, help learners:
- identify common wants and interests effortlessly;
- compliment, praise and congratulate convincingly;
- express remorse and sympathy genuinely;
- negotiate and exchange ideas naturally;
- minimise misunderstandings quickly;
- defend themselves and their opinions respectfully;
- analyse, propose and reflect comfortably;
- interrupt politely;
- and above all … participate confidently in conversation.

This list, though not exclusive, all suggests mastery.

To get there, a good place to start is with roleplays and case studies – to introduce how context changes our utterances:

- Encouraging learners to share their experiences and misadventures of using English also generates lively discussion and amusement.

English language competence subsequently becomes acquired through guided *discovery*, rather than being *prescribed*:

- Formal examination bodies, too, are also coming around to the idea, by carefully reconsidering their questions and assessment criteria. We will look at assessment more in Part C.

A knowledge of pragmatics also takes intercultural understanding to a new level.

Learning pragmatics in English

'It often shows a fine command of the English language to say nothing.'
Graffiti, University of Michigan [58]

See the activity **DIY gap fill** on page 46.

Something as simple as writing the word 'Hello' on the board, for example, and asking the learners to list all the alternatives they know in written or spoken English can already start them on a path to understanding:

– how English changes according to formality (*Good afternoon, 'Sup?*);

See the activity **Adjacency pairs** on page 54.

– how English changes according to the number of people being addressed (*Ladies and Gentlemen* is usual, but *(young) lady* is an admonishment; *M'lady* probably belongs in fiction, and nobody speaking to a single man would address him as *gentleman*;

– how English differs from region to region (*G'day, Wotcha*);

See the activity **Hello, goodbye** on page 50.

– how English is used to establish friendship with people of other religions or speakers of other languages by including phrases from those languages (*As-salamu'alaykum, ¿Qué pasa?*);

– how a difference in power between the speakers changes (*Dear Sir, Alright, mate*).

For the purposes of this book, we have used the strategies listed by Brown and Levinson [59] to order the activities in Part B into separate chapters, with the aim to help our learners develop their pragmatic, as well as their linguistic, competence.

These are, after a first chapter of short introductory activities (Chapter One: 'English is context') and a second chapter from a more general perspective (Chapter Two: 'English in context'):

Chapter Three: Being direct – bald on record

Chapter Four: Being liked – positive politeness

Chapter Five: Being respected – negative politeness

Chapter Six: Being indirect – off record

The activities in Part B of *English is Context* each attempt to maximise our learners' ability to use English in contexts – by scratching only the surface of pragmatic competence, while providing the opportunity for further study and development.

References

1. Ortega y Gasset, J *Obras Completas Vol. I* Ed. Taurus/Fundación José Ortega y Gasset, Madrid 2004
2. Example given by B. Thomas (personal communication, Algeciras, Spain, February 2000)
3. Leech, G *Principles of Pragmatics* Longman Group Ltd 1983
4. Thornbury, S 'G is for Grice (and his Maxims)' *scottthornbury.wordpress.com* 2010
5. Goldstone, J (Producer), Jones, T (Director) *Monty Python's Life of Brian* (Motion picture) HandMade Films Python (Monty) Pictures Orion Pictures 1979
6. Kazanjian, H (Producer), Marquand, R (Director) *Return of the Jedi* (Motion picture) Lucasfilm Ltd 1983
7. Gell-Mann, M and Ruhlen, M 'The origin and evolution of word order' Proceedings of the National Academy of Sciences (PNAS) 2011
8. Milne, A A *The House at Pooh Corner* Methuen & Co. Ltd 1928
9. Hallo, W W *The World's Oldest Literature: Studies in Sumerian Belles-Lettres* Koninklijke Brill NV 2010 Also: *https://www.britannica.com/topic/Sicilian-mimes*
10. *Ibid.*
11. Nietzsche, F *Human, All Too Human* (Hollingdale R J, Transl.) Cambridge University Press 1966 (Original work published 1878)
12. *https://www.britannica.com/topic/Sicilian-mimes* (*op. cit.*)
13. 'Instructions of Shuruppak' from Lambert W G *Babylonian Wisdom Literature* Eisenbrauns, Winona Lake, Indiana 1996 (Includes online English translation)
14. Dawkins, R *The Blind Watchmaker: Why the Evidence of Evolution Reveals a Universe Without Design* Norton & Company Inc 1986
15. Loeb Classical Library, Harvard University Press, Vol. XXI 1913 (Latin text with facing English translation by Walter Miller)
16. Heine, H *Complete Poetical Works* (Bowring E A, Transl.) Delphi 2016
17. Wilde, O *The Canterville Ghost* J. W. Luce and Company 1906 (Reprint Harvard University 2006)
18. Fox, K *Watching the English* (2nd edn) Hodder & Stoughton 2014
19. House, J, Kasper, G and Ross, S *Misunderstanding in Social Life: Discourse Approaches to Problematic Talk* Routledge 2014
20. Sartre, J-P 'L'écrivain est en situation dans son époque: chaque parole a des retentissements. Chaque silence aussi.' *Les Temps Modernes: Revue Mensuelle* 1 (1) 1945
21. Shakespeare, W *Henry IV Part 2* Ed. Penguin UK 2005 (Believed to have been written between 1596 and 1599)
22. O'Farrell, J *An Utterly Impartial History of Britain – or 2000 years of Upper Class Idiots in Charge* Transworld Digital 4 September 2008 (First published in Great Britain Doubleday 2007)
23. Crystal, D *Let's Talk: How English Conversation Works* Oxford University Press 2020
24. Shakespeare, W *Henry IV Part 2* (*op. cit.*)
25. *www.etymonline.com*
26. Wodehouse, P G *My Man Jeeves* Editorium 2008 (Original work written 1919)
27. Wright, M *The Art of Conversation and How to Apply Its Technique* Whittlesey 1936
28. Sherman, R (Producer), Peckinpah, S (Director) *Convoy* (Motion picture) EMI Films 1978
29. Halliday, M A K 'Anti-Languages' *American Anthropologist* American Anthropological Association 1976
30. Austin, J L 'How to do things with words' The William James Lectures, delivered at Harvard University 1955
31. Wittgenstein, L 'Philosophical Investigations I, 43 and 71' Translation: John Wiley & Sons 2010
32. Austin, J L 'How to do things with words' The William James Lectures, delivered at Harvard University (*op. cit.*)
33. Austin, J L 'A Plea for Excuses' Proceedings of the Aristotelian Society, New Series Vol. 57 (1956–1957) Published by Blackwell on behalf of The Aristotelian Society

References

34 Larson, D attributed to *Doug's Dugout* Green Bay Press-Gazette 1964–1988

35 Carroll, L (Charles L. Dodgson) *Alice in Wonderland and Through the Looking-glass* Wordsworth Classics 1991 (First published 1872)

36 Grice, P 'Logic and conversation' In Cole, P and Morgan, J (Eds) *Syntax and Semantics 3 – Speech acts* New York: Academic Press 1975

37 Pinker, S 'The evolutionary social psychology of off-record indirect speech acts' (Paper) Harvard University 2007

38 Leech, G *Principles of Pragmatics* (*op. cit.*)

39 Goffman, E 'On Face-Work: An Analysis of Ritual Elements in Social Interaction' *Psychiatry* 18 (3) 1955

40 Chanel, G B In Spivack, E 'Top 10 Chanelisms: Coco's Wise Words to Mark Her Birthday' *smithsonianmag.com* 2010

41 *The Saga of the Völsungs – The Norse Epic of Sigurd the Dragon Slayer* Penguin Books 2013

42 Brown, P and Levinson, S *Politeness: Universals in Language Usage* Cambridge University Press 1987 (First published as part of Esther N Goody (Ed) *Questions and Politeness* Cambridge University Press 1978)

43 Hollett, V 'Politeness' Posted in LEARNING TO SPEAK 'MERICAN (blog) *merican.vickihollett.com* 2009

44 Hu-Chan, M *Saving Face: How to Preserve Dignity and Build Trust* Berrett-Koehler Publishers 2020

45 John Lydon (aka Johnny Rotten) Interview *The Filth and the Fury* Prior to the Sex Pistols' North American tour 2003 *https://www.johnlydon.com/interviews/usa2003.html*

46 Culpeper, J *Impoliteness: Using Language to Cause Offence* Cambridge University Press 2011

47 Abrams, E '*'There are no dirty words, only dirty minds*' – *The Altamont Enterprise*' The official website of Lenny Bruce *lennybruce.org* 2020

48 Wilson, D and Sperber, D 'Relevance Theory' *UCL Psychology and Language Sciences* (Paper available as a pdf) 2002
Sperber, D and Wilson D *Relevance: Communication and Cognition* Harvard University Press 1986

49 Vygotsky, L S and Cole, M *Mind in Society: Development of Higher Psychological Processes* Harvard University Press 1978

50 Goffman, E 'On Face-Work: An Analysis of Ritual Elements in Social Interaction' (*op. cit.*)

51 Brown, P and Levinson, S *Politeness: Universals in Language Usage* (*op. cit.*)

52 Culpeper, J *Journal of Pragmatics* (*op. cit.*)

53 Montessori, M *The Montessori Method: The Origins of an Educational Innovation: Including an Abridged and Annotated Edition of Maria Montessori's The Montessori Method* Rowman & Littlefield 2004

54 Lessing, D *The Four-Gated City* MacGibbon & Kee 1969

55 Bardovi-Harlig, K 'Pragmatics and language teaching: Bringing pragmatics and pedagogy together' *Pragmatics and Language Learning* 7 1996

56 Chomsky, N *Aspects of the Theory of Syntax* The MIT Press 1965

57 Variously attributed: first to Socrates, then to Plutarch and, much later, to W. B. Yeats.

58 Reisner, R and Wechsler, L University of Michigan *Encyclopedia of Graffiti* Macmillan 1974

59 Brown, P and Levinson, S *Politeness: Universals in Language Usage* (*op. cit.*)

Recommended reading

If you would like to read more, we can certainly recommend the following:

The Lexicographer's Dilemma: The Evolution of 'Proper' English, from Shakespeare to South Park
by Jack Lynch
(Walker Books 2013)

The Oxford Handbook of Pragmatics
by Yan Huang
(Oxford University Press 2019)

Discourse Analysis for Language Teachers
by Michael McCarthy
(Cambridge University Press 1991)

History of English
by Jonathan Culpeper
(Routledge 2015)

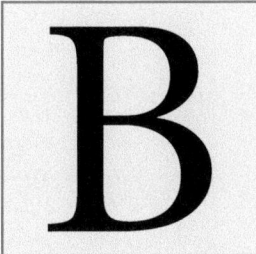

English as Context will now provide practical activities to help your learners improve their pragmatic competence.

Starting with some short introductory tasks, followed by a very general look at the relationship between language and context, we will then move on to the more specific strategies of politeness theory.

- **Chapter One** presents 20 mini-activities, which can act as warmers (or appetisers) at the beginning of a lesson to encourage your learners to consider the language they use – or at the end, to get them thinking in preparation for the next lesson.
- **Chapter Two** takes the language that your learners are likely to encounter in their environment – media, songs, literature – and encourages them to consider how context can, and will, change the meaning of the very same words.
- **Chapter Three** focuses on the first of the politeness strategies – 'bald on record', according to Brown and Levinson in *Politeness: Universals in Language Usage* (see page 24 in Part A) – and looks at **direct** statements where language is taken at face value and where the minimum number of words necessary to communicate a message clearly may be (mis)interpreted as a personal affront.
- **Chapter Four** concentrates on 'in group' language – jargon and slang – and building rapport through empathy and humour. The **'positive politeness'** strategy aims to make speakers feel good about themselves and be liked by others.
- **Chapter Five** includes the strategy of **'negative politeness'** – not to be confused with *impoliteness* – which means attempting to maintain respect, by using tact and sensitivity as well as other ways to minimise any imposition. Depending on the culture in which this strategy is used, it can appear to be either perfectly normal – or insincere.
- **Chapter Six** deals with the confusing 'off record' and avoidance strategies that depend on the hearer being able to make sense of the speaker's **indirect** use of words to express something different from what they mean – using and recognising sarcasm and irony, changes in meaning through intonation and expressions that are either unexpected or appear contradictory.

But before we move on to these activities, we suggest a 'Politeness Quiz' to get your learners thinking about the strategies they are most comfortable with – in a series of ten situations.

This quiz can also act as a useful reference for you when introducing your class to the different approaches that we use when speaking to others.

This icon indicates where some of the resources that support and complement the activities have been placed on the DELTA website for you to download for your convenience.

Simply register at www.deltapublishing.co.uk and search for the ISBN 501742 to access the downloadable material.

How are you polite?

Raising awareness of personal politeness strategies

Strategy
Identifying learners' individual approaches and the language they prefer to use, depending on the context.

Setting the context
This is not a quiz about how *polite* learners are but – as the title says – *how* they are polite:
- In other words, it encourages them to reflect on the approaches or strategies that they would be most comfortable using in different contexts.

By comparing their answers, the learners recognise that we each adopt different ways to get what we want.

Instead of making sweeping judgements about how we communicate – eg 'the Germans/French are rude; introverted engineers look at their shoes when talking to you, extroverted engineers look at *your* shoes – the learners contemplate how the language we choose leads to misunderstandings.

Setting up
○ Prepare a copy of the Quiz – on page 37, or downloaded from the website – for each learner.

○ Prepare copies of the Key on page 38 if you have decided to hand it out:
- You may prefer to limit the information in the Key – according to your class and your lesson objectives – in which case, you can simply refer to the Key summary.

Step by step
- Ask the learners about any differences or misunderstandings they have noticed when dealing with other cultures, or when travelling:
  - *What do they think were the reasons for these?*
  - *Do they blame themselves for not having sufficient cultural awareness?*
  - *Or was something else at play?*

- Tell them that you have a Quiz to help them identify how we all use different strategies to get what we want.

- Give them a copy of the Quiz – and time to answer:
  - If they would not say anything in a particular situation, they do not need to make a selection.
  - Explain that sometimes they might add a reason for saying something.

- Once they have finished, and before referring to the Key, ask them to compare their answers:
  - *Why did they choose the answers they did?*
  - *Were their answers mostly A, B, C or D?*
  - *Which, if any, did they not respond to?*
  - *What differences do they notice between the answers for A, B, C and D?*

- Read the Key together – or tell the learners what each choice in the answers represents:
  - *Does the Key match what they said about the different categories?*
  - *What evidence can they find in the Quiz for what the Key says?*

- Ask the learners if they agree with their own results:
  - *Do they think that the groupings tell them anything about their cultures (regional, corporate, status, etc) or those of others?*
  - *Do the results help them to understand why and how other people or cultures behave?*

- Ask them:
  - *Can they share any personal stories of a misunderstanding which might have happened as a consequence of the different strategies used by the speakers?*

Signing off
You can give the learners some sample imperatives, or 'bald on record' statements, and ask them to make these fit the strategies listed in the Key. For example:
- 'Shut up!' –
  - *Let's enjoy some silence for a moment.*
    (Being liked – positive politeness)
  - *Do you think you could listen and not comment?*
    (Being respected – negative politeness)
  - *You look beautiful with your mouth closed.*
    (Being indirect – off record)
- 'Go away!' –
  - *We should go our separate ways.* (positive)
  - *Perhaps you should go.* (negative)
  - *Sling your hook.* (off record)

Ask the learners to compile phrase lists from their everyday correspondence or exposure to English, and to come up with alternatives for the strategies listed in the Key.

Politeness strategies

In context

Read the situations below, and select the suggested phrase that you prefer.
Sometimes, you may follow it with an explanation of why you are saying this.
If you would prefer to say nothing in a situation, there is no need to make a selection.

1 Someone speaks with an unusual accent, and you want them to repeat what they've just said. You say …
   - A What did you say?
   - B Run that by me again.
   - C Sorry, could you repeat that?
   - D My hearing isn't so good.

2 You are taking an exam in a hot and stuffy room. You summon the invigilator, and you say …
   - A Open the window.
   - B Could we open a window?
   - C Would it be possible to have a window opened?
   - D It's very hot in here.

3 You want to write a sign to tell visitors to your office not to smoke. You write …
   - A No smoking!
   - B Thank you for not smoking.
   - C Smoking not permitted in this office.
   - D Smoking kills!

4 You are in a meeting, and disagree with what someone says. You want to interrupt, so you say …
   - A Wait, I have a question!
   - B You're making an excellent point, but can I just jump in?
   - C I'm sorry, I have to disagree …
   - D How did you come to that conclusion?

5 You know that your boss is not happy about the job you are doing. You say …
   - A What's wrong?
   - B If you tell me what I'm doing wrong, I'm sure we can work this out.
   - C Do you think you could help me understand what I'm doing wrong?
   - D I can see you're not happy …

6 A friend tells you that they have recently been made redundant. You say …
   - A Don't worry – you'll soon find another job.
   - B How sad – can I do anything to help?
   - C Have you tried applying for other jobs?
   - D There are plenty more fish in the sea.

7 You are going to the airport to catch a plane, but the bus is very crowded. You want other passengers to make room, so you say …
   - A Move!
   - B If we move up a bit, we can all get there.
   - C I don't suppose you could make room for one more?
   - D I'm late for my plane!

8 You are in the queue at a busy supermarket, and the person behind you is standing too close for comfort. You say …
   - A Keep your distance!
   - B Let's give each other some space, mate.
   - C Would you mind standing a little further away?
   - D We don't want to step on each other's toes.

9 You have told your neighbour that you are going away for a few days. You would like him/her to water your plants, so you say …
   - A Remember to water the plants.
   - B It would be great if you watered my plants.
   - C Do you think you could water my plants?
   - D I'm worried about my begonias.

10 Some colleagues have just told you that they are going to have lunch together. You would like to join them, so you say …
   - A I'm coming too!
   - B I'll join you, if that's alright with everyone.
   - C Would it be alright if I joined you?
   - D Now you mention it, I'm hungry, too.

Politeness strategies

Key

This task intends only to draw attention to the strategies we often prefer to use, and why we use them. It is not a guide to decide which type of person or learner we are.

A:
These responses could be considered too direct for many people, or even impolite. Such directness is only really suitable for close relationships where: the speakers know each other well enough not to worry about making a favourable impression; or perhaps they toy with giving a minimal response; or where the matter is of utmost urgency and an immediate warning is necessary.

Such directness is linguistically known as being **bald on record**.

B:
These responses help the speaker to be liked and be included in the hearer's social group, a strategy known as **positive politeness***.

The speaker attempts to use 'in' words, crack a joke, speak in terms of being 'in this together' or demonstrate empathy with a situation. The speaker needs to tread carefully, though, as it could backfire. An inappropriate choice of topic or address, or a lack of cultural awareness, could lead to offence or an immediate loss of respect.

C:
These responses are more concerned with helping the speaker to maintain respect and minimise any imposition, rather than being liked or included in a group. They use 'hedges', 'fuzzy language' and pessimism – distancing the speaker with passives and generalisations (preferring *one* to *you*). Too much of it, however, will be unnatural for many contexts and can make the speaker appear arrogant.

This strategy is known as **negative politeness***.

D:
These responses avoid saying anything directly, to protect the speaker. Using metaphor or idiom to suggest or imply what they are thinking, the speaker depends on the hope that the hearer will be able to interpret what they say and understand what *is* – or in this case *isn't* – said.

While being **off record** can lead to misunderstandings, it also allows the speaker to claim all innocence if their utterances lead to potential conflict.

No response:
The speaker avoids the situation entirely, in order to avoid any embarrassment.

This might be seen as weak, or having a lack of confidence, but it could equally be the case that the speaker sees no point in saying anything, if they think that the hearer will ignore them anyway.

---

* The terms *positive* and *negative politeness* are used by linguists simply to express that they are opposite polarities, in the same way that magnets have positive and negative fields. The terms do not mean that one is good and one is bad.

Key summary

The fundamental strategies are these:

A: Being direct – Bald on record.
B: Being liked – Positive politeness.
C: Being respected – Negative politeness.
D: Being indirect – Off record.
No response: The speaker avoids the situation.

Chapter One

English is context

Do you want to know a secret?

For a great many learners – and for quite a lot of teachers too – pragmatics is one of the best-kept secrets of language learning.

Letting that cat out of the bag will lead to plenty of 'a-ha!' moments – where learners begin to understand the connection between what speakers *say* and the words they *use*.

This first chapter of short activities covers a wide range of contexts and concepts in an endeavour to open the eyes and whet the appetite to learn more – on the staircase leading to pragmatic competence.

This is just the beginning.

Prepare to be surprised – a short activity may spontaneously develop into a prolonged and creative discussion.

Such is the potential of *context*!

Howyis!

Getting to grips with greetings

Strategy

Interpreting the moods or frames of mind of others in initial greetings.

Step by step

- Ask your learners the question *'How are you?'* and try to elicit some different responses.
- Write these on the board.
- Add any of the responses below if they have not already been mentioned:
  - Not too bad.
  - Can't complain, I suppose.
  - OK.
  - Alright.
  - Alive.
  - Better than ever.
  - Better, thanks.
  - Could be worse.
  - Just peachy …
- Ask the class:
  - *How do they think the speaker is feeling in each situation?*
  - *How would they continue the conversation?*

Postscript: The length of the reply depends on how well the speakers know each other.

Sometimes, if they are merely acquaintances, the answer should be very short (*'Fine, thanks.'*), with things left at that.

Other times, *'How are you?'* may not be a question at all.

The Irish, for example, may use it as nothing more than a greeting – learners shouldn't be surprised to hear the same thing in reply:
'Howyis, Mrs Connolly!'
'Howyis, Moira!'

* See *Adjacency pairs* on page 54.

English by radio

Understanding from context

Strategy

Identifying context from key words.

Step by step

- Play a podcast, advert or news broadcast to the class in a language that the learners don't know.
- Ask them to listen out for any words they do recognise, or can guess from the context:
  - *What do they think the speaker is talking about?*
- Tell them that when listening to podcasts and Internet radio stations, watching films and series without subtitles, etc, in English …
  - Initially, because of their level, they may understand very little.
  - Recognising the *context* can help them improve their comprehension, vocabulary and even pronunciation.

Postscript: In the days before the Internet, the BBC used shortwave radio to transmit language learning classes to the world.

The service, known as *English by Radio*, eventually metamorphosed into the rich bank of online learning materials now known as *BBC Learning English*.

* See *Blame it on the boogie* on page 53.

CHAPTER ONE • ENGLISH IS CONTEXT

In the mood
Combining contexts

Strategy
Matching visual and verbal contexts.

Step by step
- Select a few lines from different texts or songs that express different emotions or feelings. For example:
  - *Here we are now, entertain us, I feel stupid and contagious.*
    (Nirvana)
  - *Oh, it's such a perfect day I'm glad I spent it with you.*
    (Lou Reed)
  - *Everybody cries, and everybody hurts sometimes.*
    (R.E.M.)
  - *When the working day is done, Oh girls, they wanna have fun.*
    (Cyndi Lauper)
- Give these to your learners:
  - *Can they find pictures that reflect these emotions?*
- Ask the learners to share their pictures with each other and explain their choices.

Postscript: English language tests, such as those offered by *Cambridge Assessment English*, often involve learners doing the opposite – having to discuss the situation behind a picture:
- how the people are feeling;
- the sounds they might be hearing;
- what happened next.

* See *Soap bubbles* on page 62.

Pick 'n' mix
Alternative contexts

Strategy
Suggesting alternative answers to a 'mix and match' exercise.

Step by step
- Tell your learners that conversation involves taking turns to listen and respond to what your partner says:
  - This is frequently reflected in coursebooks with a 'mix and match' exercise, where learners have to select parts of a sentence from two lists to complete an expression.
- Find a suitable exercise to work with, and ask the class to complete it.
- Tell the learners that the conversational pairings provided by coursebooks are often limited to one context. Working in pairs or small groups:
  - *Can they decide if any of the other choices are also possible in some contexts?*
  - *Can they come up with three further alternatives for each sentence provided in the first column or box?*
- Ask the class to share their alternatives:
  - *How specific do they think these are to context?*

Postscript: Though they are very popular in coursebooks, mix-and-match exercises may run the risk of over-simplifying, and – if no context is given – limiting flexibility in language use and creative thinking.

* See *Song lyrics roleplays* on page 57.

Classroom tickers
Summarising

Strategy
Summarising texts into short messages, and checking understanding.

Step by step
- Ask the class where they remember seeing *news tickers*, the narrow strips of information which often appear at the bottom of the screen in news channels or on the sides of buildings.
- Explain that the basic rules for writing these are:
  - limiting words to a minimum number of characters.
  - using phrases that are short and to the point.
  - avoiding the use of connecting words such as:
    articles (*a*, *the*, etc);
    pronouns (*I*, *me*, *mine*, etc);
    conjunctions (*and*, *but*, *if*, etc).
- Give the learners different texts (eg news stories or articles) to read and to summarise paragraphs for a news ticker.
- Ask them to give these to their partners, who then try to re-construct the story.

Postscript: Reading assessment tests, such as for *Cambridge Assessment English* exams, require the scanning and paraphrasing of ideas.

Candidates often lose valuable marks by not completing their sentences and not being clear – in an expectation that the reader will understand what they mean.

This activity helps learners recognise this problem.

* See *Clearing the dead wood* on page 75.

What do you suppose?
Predicting from context

Strategy
Predicting text.

Step by step
- In a class reading (and listening) exercise, read a text aloud to the class – or ask a volunteer, while the others listen.
- Every once in a while, the reader should stop and ask the class to guess what comes next.
  - *Do they expect a noun, a verb, etc?*
  - *What do they suppose comes next?*
- Once a few learners have guessed, the reader continues the text.
- When finished, ask the class:
  - *Which contextual clues (eg favourable or negative descriptions, the writer's feelings about what they wrote …) helped them to guess what came next?*

Postscript: Learners will be familiar with predictive text when sending messages on their phones.

How do they think their own ability to predict text compares with that of their trusty electronic friends?

* See *Here is the news* on page 70.

Have you Meghan Markled?
Very personal verbs

Strategy
Using names as verbs.

Step by step
- Ask the class:
  - *What companies or brand names can the learners think of that have become verbs?*
  (For example: *Google, Photoshop, Fed Ex, Xerox* …)
  - *How do these words change grammatically in the process?*
  (For example: over time and frequency of use, they become uncapitalised, and with no need for italics.)
- Tell the learners that, according to *The Guardian* newspaper, *(to) Meghan Markle* is now a verb, meaning:

  'to value yourself and your mental health enough to up and leave a room/situation/environment in which your authentic self is not welcomed or wanted.'
- Ask your learners to write down the names of about eight famous celebrities or people from history:
  - *Can they think of definitions for the names they thought of, to share with the class – as verbs?*

Postscript: Adjectives which originate from someone's name are known as eponymous adjectives and 'typically' end in *-ist, -ite, -ian, -esque* and *-ic* (eg Marxist, Jakobite, Kennedyesque, Platonic, Grundtvigian (!) …).

The phrase 'your name is mud' is believed to originate from Samuel Mudd, a physician who conspired in the assassination of Abraham Lincoln.

* See also *Word of the year* on page 48.

Taboo in role
Rhetoric

Strategy
Recognising character through rhetoric.

Step by step
- The rhetoric of people in a particular trade will vary, depending on their interests and characteristics:
  - A teacher may ask the hearer to repeat what they have been told.
  - A private detective will be more inquisitive.
  - A car salesman may try to be much more persuasive.
  - An artist or writer: dreamy.
  - A civil servant: disinterested or unhelpful.
- In a game of *Taboo*, players have to describe a word to their teams without using the word itself:
  - Here, the learners describe these words – but in the character of a particular profession.
- Select a group of words to use in the game, and divide the class into groups.
- Ask one or two members of each group to take turns to describe the words:
  - *Can the rest of their group try to guess the word and the profession?*

Postscript: The words and expressions used in a particular trade or with a special interest may either confuse – or not be understood by – those 'not in the know'.

Do your learners use such context-specific jargon during this game?

Such language need not be specialist, but can also be a cultural or regional term.

* See *Donald, Where's Your Troosers?* on page 81.

Dinner date from history
Diplomacy

Strategy
Expressing potentially sensitive or difficult topics diplomatically.

Step by step
- Tell your learners that they are going to go on a dinner date with anyone from history:
  - This can be anyone – from the person who made the first cave drawing, to someone who is a living person, but can be considered a 'historical' figure.
- Ask the learners to think about the topics they would like to discuss, and then write down a list of questions that they would like to ask:
  - They should not mention the name of the person in their questions.
- When the list of questions is complete, other classmates can then guess who the person is:
  - What do they think the answers would be?
- Reflect together on the language used to ask the questions:
  - *Did the learners write their questions in a way that would make the hearers like and connect with them, and maintain the hearers' respect – or were they being more indirect?*
  - *Can they explain why they chose this approach?*

Postscript: The British author and TV presenter Jeremy Paxman is famous for being blunt with the people he interviews, yet rarely does he seem to lose their respect.

Paxman explains that once he has compiled his questions, he must continue to 'discern' what he wants to discover – either until he receives an answer, or until it becomes clear that the person is not going to tell him.

* See *Age, sex, location?* on page 84.

Mind your Ps and Qs!
Politeness perspectives

Strategy
Recognising the difference between over-politeness and impoliteness.

Step by step
- Ask your learners to write down some examples of sentences they consider to be very polite. These could be phrases used when:
  – meeting;
  – complimenting;
  – apologising;
  – listening attentively to someone.
- Tell the learners:
  'When politeness is used to show up other people, it is reclassified as rudeness.'
  Judith Martin
- Ask the learners:
  - *Which of their phrases might be considered excessive or insincere – and consequently impolite?*

Postscript: Judith Martin, better known as Miss Manners, is an American author and etiquette agony aunt.

She has written books such as *Miss Manners' Guide to Excruciatingly Correct Behavior* and *Minding Miss Manners: In an Era of Fake Etiquette*.

Advising us that the best way to learn how to behave politely is seeing things from the other person's point of view, she says that 'learning American manners from American films is like learning traffic rules from watching car chases'.

There are several fascinating explanations as to the origin of the expression *Mind your Ps and Qs*, perhaps the most plausible being:

'Ps and Qs' – or P's and Q's – is short for *pleases* and *thank yous*, the latter containing a sound similar to the letter Q.

* See *Sorry seems to be the hardest word* on page 100.

CHAPTER ONE • ENGLISH IS CONTEXT

Afflicted with sarcasm
Intonation

Strategy
Identifying clues in intonation and pitch to understand the speaker's point of view.

Step by step
- Ask your learners how good they think they are at telling whether a speaker is being sincere:
  - ☐ Which clues help them?
    - Are these visual or contextual only?
    - Do they think that there may also be linguistic clues?
- Write the sentences below on the board and ask the learners to read them aloud.
- They should try to change the intonation, so that they sound sarcastic:
  - I enjoy listening to Celine Dion's (or musician of your choice) music; it's moving.
  - The weather at this time of year is wonderful.
  - I'm interested in astrology.
  - Facebook is a good way to stay in touch with friends.
  - (Name of famous person) is a brilliant footballer/politician/speaker.
- Ask the learners:
  - ☐ How can adding qualifiers (eg really, absolutely, so, wonderful) change how the sentences above are understood in context?
  - ☐ Which of these do the class think add to the in/sincerity of what is said?

Postscript: The British comedians David Baddiel and Robert Newman created a character called Ray, a man who was afflicted with a 'disease' – whatever he said or however sincerely he meant it, everything came out sounding sarcastic.

Find some videos of Ray on *YouTube* and show these to your learners.

* See *Ambiguous appraisals* on page 111.

Thinking outside the box
Context from language

Strategy
Deducing context from language.

Step by step
- In job interviews or aptitude tests, candidates may be asked questions that test their ability to use their imagination and their ability to think outside the box. For example:
  - *Why are many manhole covers round?*
    (Answer: because their shape prevents them from falling down circular pipes.)
  - *How many uses can you think of for a potato, other than cooking and eating it?*
    (Answer: potato prints, removing stains or a broken lightbulb from a socket, etc.)
- Ask your learners the above questions and discuss the answers – to get them thinking 'creatively'.
- To encourage the learners' aptitude for using language creatively, ask them to find as many different contexts for phrases that they are already familiar with. For example:
  - *The paper was exceptional.*
    (Was *'the paper'* an essay, a sketchbook, something that was flushed down the toilet …?)
  - *So what's in it for me?*
    (Is *'it'* a project, a food, a tombola or raffle …?)
  - *No matter how hard I try, I just can't pick it up!*
    (Does *'pick up'* mean to gather or learn? Is *'it'* an object, or a skill such as speaking a language?)

Postscript: This activity can be a good way to visualise, and practise, phrasal verbs, which often have several meanings – eg *take off* (become airborne, depart quickly, be a sudden success), *run out* (leave, use up, expire, extend), etc.

* See *Reading between the lines* on page 115.

CHAPTER ONE • ENGLISH IS CONTEXT

DIY gap fill
Vocabulary into context

Strategy
Finding words for contexts.

Step by step
- Give your learners one strip of paper each, with an individual word of your choice on one side.
- On the other side, ask them to write one sentence, putting the word into any context they wish, but leaving a gap where the word should be.
- Ask them to show their sentences to the rest of the class:
  - *Can they guess what the missing word is?*

Postscript: This task is useful to review vocabulary from a previous lesson – it helps your learners not just to remember the word itself, but the context in which is used.

Learners will often create vocabulary lists, including nothing but individual words and perhaps a translation.

Remind them that *context* can change meaning, and encourage them to write sample *sentences* when recording new words.

* See *It's gobbledygook to me!* on page 123

Circumstantial synonyms
Context from vocabulary

Strategy
Deducing context from vocabulary.

Step by step
- Before setting a reading comprehension exercise, select five or six words from the text that do not immediately appear to be related to the topic:
  - In a report of a football game, for example, you might find the following words:
  flash, *chariot*, *shot*, *blues* and *costly*.
- Before telling the class what the article is about, give the learners these words and ask them to discuss what they think the text is about.
- As they read:
  - *When they come across the words, can they explain the connection between the words and the story?*

Postscript: The *Oxford English Dictionary* has more than 290,000 entries, which not only makes English one of the largest languages by word count but probably also the language with the largest numbers of synonyms.

The word with the most number of meanings according to the *Guinness Book of Records* – 'set' – has 430 senses listed.

* See *Reading between the lines* on page 115.

Article of faith
The definite article in context

Strategy
Recognising the pragmatic functions of the definite article.

Step by step
- Ask your learners to write on a card any sentence which includes the definite article.
- On the board, write the following sentences, and ask the class where they think these lines might come from, or who might have said them:
  1 *The Irish are superstitious.*
  2 *Join the Club/Society for the Prevention of Santa Denial.*
  3 *The Rock Hotel is the hotel on the island.*
- Tell the class that in the examples above:
  1 This uses the definite article to distance or exclude the speaker from the subject; and it is probably spoken – a headline, for example, would omit the article.
  2 There was no such club/society until the article created or introduced it.
  3 This phrase comes from a promotional billboard. Depending on intonation, it implies:
     – either there is only one hotel on the island;
     – or this hotel is the best;
     – or it is one of several hotels in different places.
- Ask the learners:
  ☐ *What does the article in the sentences they wrote earlier tell us about the context?*

Postscript: As well as being *the* only definite article in English, 'the' is also the most commonly used word.

It can be used with singular and plural words, words that start with any letter, and does not change according to case.

Its many functions include: to introduce, indicate, specify, classify and name – making it extremely context-dependent.

* See *Daley Starr* on page 94.

Swings and roundabouts
Yes or no – or neither?

Strategy
Using alternatives to yes and no.

Step by step
- This is an old game where players try to catch each other out by answering questions – but have to avoid saying *yes* or *no*.
- Ask individual learners to take turns, with a time limit of one minute, at answering questions asked by either you as teacher, or by the class.
- The learners must respond orally (they cannot nod or shake their heads):
  ☐ If they say *yes* or *no* they are out of the game.
- Are the responses:
  – Conditional (*It could be …*)?
  – Adverbs (*Perhaps, Possibly, etc*)?
  – A reciprocal question (*What do you think? Why not?*)?
  – Indirect statements (*Many believe that to be the case*)?
- Make a note of these and reflect upon them later.
  ☐ *Which are friendly or blunt?*
  ☐ *What makes them so?*
  ☐ *Do the responses perform a function (eg stalling, quietening, changing the subject, etc)?*

Postscript: The expression 'swings and roundabouts' refers to a situation where you neither win nor lose.

A direct *yes* or *no* can be too 'definite' for many cultures.

Some will think that a 'no' is too impolite and leads to a loss of respect – and not having a mutually understood alternative can mean trouble.

Others may be advised by business gurus to not say *yes* immediately and to win a better deal – but if you are not quick off the mark, you could lose out to a rival.

* See *Avoidance charades* on page 114.

So there!

Short words with multiple uses

Strategy
The versatility and functions of *so*, *there* and other short exclamations.

Step by step
- Write the words 'so' and 'there' on the board.
- Ask the learners to think of the different uses of these words, and to write some example sentences. Some suggested uses are:
  - So, what's for lunch?
  - I was so hungry.
  - So am I!
  - How are you? Oh, so so.
  - He was such a so and so.
  - So there!
  - So what?
  - There you go.
  - There, there, there.
  - There now.
  - Hello there.
- Ask the class to share their sentences.
- Write an example of each use on the board, adding any from the above list:
  - □ *How is 'so' and 'there' used in each example?*
  - □ *What function do they serve (eg to start a sentence, comfort, complain, etc)?*
  - □ *Can the learners think of any other short words (conjunctions, adverbs, etc) that have different meanings or functions (eg look, well, OK, really)?*

Postscript: 'So' has become ever-present in everyday conversation and its meaning can change, depending on where in the sentence it appears.

It can be used to *start* a sentence, to *end* a sentence, or be left dangling in the *middle*, with an expectation that the hearer will guess what the speaker is suggesting.

Consider the differences between:
So you're right.
You're so right.
You're right, so …

* See *Mark my words* on page 116.

Word of the year

Contemporary vocabulary

Strategy
Understanding usage by comparing local varieties of English.

Step by step
- Each year, most major dictionaries (Oxford, Macquarie, Merriam-Webster …) select one word that reflects either an important event or a social trend in the year that was. This word is designated the 'Word of the Year'.
- Search online for lists of either current or previous 'words of the year' and ask:
  - □ *How does language reflect the times in which we live?* (See the Postscript below.)
- The *American Dialect Society* has the following categories for its list:
  - The most useful.
  - The most creative.
  - The most outrageous.
  - The most euphemistic.
  - The most and least likely to succeed.
- Ask your learners to think about the English words they know.
  - □ *What are their favourite words for each of the above categories?*

Postscript: Though the tradition of choosing a 'word of the year', or *Wort des Jahres*, was started by the Germans (*Gesellschaft für deutsche Sprache* – German Language Association) in 1971, the idea was first adopted in the English language in 1990 by the *American Dialect Society*.

That year, the US President, George H W Bush, had broken the promise he made two years before when he told the nation to 'Read my lips: no new taxes'.

The word chosen was *Bushlips* – meaning a stupid or untrue remark.

* See *A taboo U-turn* on page 122.

On the slur of the moment

Character insinuations and insults

Strategy
Recognising and avoiding offensive slurs.

Step by step
- Write the following on the board:
  - party pooper
  - right winger
  - tree-hugger
  - fuddy-duddy
  - old-timer
  - wino
  - riffraff
  - gold digger
  - cowboy
  - pen pusher
- Ask your learners to explain what kind of people they describe:
  - *Can they think of any words to describe the opposite of the above (eg party animal, spring chicken, fat cat …)?*
- Explain that all of these are character slurs – terms which classify according to interests or habits – often with an intention to dismiss or shame:
  - *Which do they think are socially acceptable?*
  - *Which not?*
  - *Why?*
- Why do the class think we use such slurs?
  - *Is it to criticise and offend?*
  - *Or to establish membership and camaraderie within a group?*

Postscript: Words such as *weirdo*, *junkie* and *geek* may originally have been intended as insults, but they have been adopted as affectionate terms for those:
- who rebel against convention:
  (being a *weirdo* instead of a *plain Jane/average Joe* …)
- who are enthusiasts of a particular hobby such as blogs and forums:
  (*tefleek.net*; *BoardGameGeek* …)
- who just can't get enough of something:
  (*adrenalin junkies*, *space junkies* …)

* See *A royal bastard* on page 80.

Emoji translators

Visualising words

Strategy
Translating text to graphical representations.

Step by step
- Ask your class how they feel about using:
  - emojis – images such as smileys ☺
  - emoticons – images from keyboard characters **:-)**
- Ask the learners:
  - *Do they use these only in informal communication?*
  - *Would they also use them in more formal contexts, such as in business emails?*
  - *Do they use them more, or less, than in the past few years?*
- Ask them:
  - *How do they understand different emojis?*
  - *How have they used them?*
  - The *Pile of Poo* – 💩 – emoji may be used as an expletive, but is also used as a symbol of good luck:
    The Japanese words for poo (*unko*) and luck (*un*) start with the same sound.
- Give the learners some example sentences:
  - *Can they translate as much of them as possible to emojis?*
  - The King James version of the Bible has been converted to emojis:
    In the beginning 😇 *created the* ✨ *and the* 🌍.
    (Genesis 1.1.)
- After a short time limit, ask the learners to share their sentences with the rest of the class.

Postscript: In 2017, an international translation company in London employed Business Psychology graduate Keith Broni as 'the world's first emoji translation expert'.

As part of his job interview, he was asked to participate in a conversion contest (the 'Emoji Spelling Bee') similar to this activity.

Keith's subsequent projects have included:
- An *Emoji Etiquette Guide*, to help people avoid emoji-based mis-communication and cross-cultural *faux pas*.
- Consulting on the use of emojis in marketing.
- An interpretation of emojis in a legal context.

* See *Literally figurative* on page 119.

Dot dot dot, dash dash dash
Punctuation in text

Strategy
Using punctuation in text messages.

Step by step
- Ask your class how they use punctuation in their text messages:
  - *Is this different to how they would use it when writing essays or letters, for example?*
- Write the following examples on the board:
  - What on earth is going on?!?
  - It's Sunday!?!
  - Will you PLEASE listen!
  - Guess what …
  - See you at 7pm.
- Ask the class:
  - *What is the effect of repeating an exclamation mark or a question mark, or putting exclamation and question marks together?*
  - *When do they use …*
    - *… (ellipses)?*
    - *' ' (inverted commas)?*
    - *ABC (capital letters) in messages?*
  - *Why?*
  - *Does a full stop (or period) at the end of a sentence make it an order – or perhaps mean that the writer does not wish to discuss the subject any further?*

Postscript: David Crystal says that texting is a 'linguistic phenomenon which has aroused curiosity, suspicion, fear, confusion, antagonism, fascination, excitement and enthusiasm, all at once'.

See: Crystal, D *Txtng: The Gr8 Db8* OUP 2008.

Much of this relies on the texter's use of punctuation, which has both the power to be brutally frank – at the same time as innocently misleading.

* See *Cannibalistic commas* on page 65.

Hello, goodbye
The appropriacy of alternatives

Strategy
Recognising the context of common expressions.

Step by step
- Tell the learners that Gibraltar, a British dependency next to Spain, is possibly the only place in the English speaking world where two friends may greet one another by saying 'goodbye' – if they are both on their way somewhere, and have no time to stop and chat.
- Write the following expressions in a row across the board:

  Hello   Yes   No   Thank you   Goodbye

- Ask the class to suggest any alternatives that they know for these. These could include formal and informal expressions:

  Hi   Absolutely   Much obliged   Yours faithfully

- Ask where and how these would be used:
  - 'Yours faithfully' is used to sign off in written correspondence – but may be seen as archaic or far too formal by some cultures.
- Write all your learners' expressions under the word for which it is a synonym:
  - *It does not matter how informal or colloquial they are.*
- Once you have a full board, ask the learners which expressions are appropriate for different people and contexts:
  - *Are there any they would never use?*
  - *Why?*

Postscript: When learners encounter authentic varieties of English outside the classroom, they soon pick up the colloquial expressions they hear.

This can lead to problems if they are not aware of the (in)appropriacy of these words – 'register' – for different situations.

Ask your learners to share with the class examples of the English they hear, and discuss how and when they were used.

* See *Simile, please!* on page 86.

Chapter Two

English in context

Here, there and everywhere

Before delving into the individual politeness strategies that we adopt, it is important to first consider how language 'behaves' – changes – depending on the context.

The activities in this chapter, therefore, aim to encourage learners to take a look at the 'big picture' and reflect on the factors that influence our choice of words and phrases.

Learners are reminded that what we *say* very often does not equal what we *mean*.

They begin by looking at what is already familiar – then reflect on the associations that they already make, and ask:

*'But what does it all **really** mean?'*

The chapter introduces *implied* meaning – known as 'implicature' – rather than what is stated literally: how this relies on understanding from context, and how meaning can be (mis)interpreted by others.

Learners see how the same words and phrases carry associations, may be perceived as favourable or unfavourable to the subject, or may change entirely in meaning – depending on context.

CHAPTER TWO • ENGLISH IN CONTEXT

Only half the story!

Being clear, relevant and orderly

Strategy
Cancelling generalisations.

Setting the context
The job of technical writers, as they will tell you in defence of their role, is to make things 'idiot-proof'!

Whether we read their instructions or not, just about everything we buy has them:
- from how to cook rice …
- to where to find the crankcase ventilation valve in your brand new car (as John Harold Haynes, founder of the extremely popular Haynes car maintenance manuals, and possibly one of the most successful technical writers ever, discovered to his delight).

Technical writers – or technical communicators, as they often like to be called – need to consider every detail and potential 'misunderstanding', when writing how-to-use guides.

If they fail to do this, or if a translation into one language does not work as it might in another, such an error immediately falls prey to the mirth of the World Wide Web.

To prevent any such 'misunderstandings' and in the interest of absolute clarity, a globally-known manufacturer of flat-pack furniture has recognised the problems that language can cause.

It has done away with words altogether in its instructions.

Setting up
Prepare a general knowledge quiz like the one opposite.

Step by step
- Explain that generalisations lead to confusion, especially when we expect the hearer to 'know' what we mean:
  - *The Swiss flag is a red square …*
    expects the hearer to already know that there is more.
  - Adding *It contains a white cross …*
    cancels the notion that the flag is entirely red.
- Ask the class about any writing that they do:
  - *How important is it for them to specify details exactly?*
  - *Do they think the reader will always understand what it is that they refer to?*

Quiz

1. *English is a Germanic language.*
   (But it has been influenced greatly by non-Germanic languages such as French and Latin. Or: But it has many borrowings from around the world.)
2. *Liverpool is a football team from Merseyside.*
   (But there are others: Everton and Tranmere.)
3. *Honda is the most popular car in Canada.*
   (But the company is Japanese.)
4. *Russia is in Europe.*
   (But a large part of the country is also in Asia.)
5. *Glasgow is the largest city in Scotland.*
   (But Edinburgh is the capital.)
6. *Passion cake is made from carrots.*
   (And flower, eggs, sugar, etc.)
7. *James Bond has been played by Daniel Craig.*
   (As well as Roger Moore, Sean Connery, etc.)
8. *The first Star Wars film was made in 1977.*
   (But it was Part IV of the series.)
9. *Herpetology is the zoological study of amphibians.*
   (But also reptiles.)
10. *The RMS Titanic set sail from Southampton in 1912.*
    (Although she was built in Belfast, Northern Ireland.)

- In teams, give your learners your general knowledge quiz:
  - *Can they add more detail – so that the hearer gets the complete picture and there is no misunderstanding?*
- At the end of the quiz, ask the class to revisit an example of some writing that they have done for you:
  - *Can they identify where they perhaps assumed that you/the reader knew what they were talking about?*
- Discuss together the dangers of too many assumptions.

Signing off
Ask your learners to write instructions for something they use every day – this will further encourage them to be clear, relevant and orderly.

To help them, you may want to provide some pictorial instructions, and ask them to provide the words (or if they enjoy drawing, do the opposite – give them the *words*).

CHAPTER TWO • ENGLISH IN CONTEXT

Blame it on the boogie

Matching contexts

Strategy
Increasing fluency by including familiar expressions from song lyrics in everyday conversation.

Setting the context
Most of us will know at least some of the words to popular songs. Sometimes this song may be in another language – and we still know the words, but not necessarily their meaning. For example:

– *Yo no soy marinero, soy capitán* (Spanish for *'I am not a sailor, I'm a captain'* from *La Bamba*)

– *Wir fahren auf der Autobahn* (German for *'We're driving on the motorway'* from *Autobahn*)

– *Je t'aime … Moi non plus* (French for *'I love you … Nor do I'* from the song of the same name)

– 오빤 강남스타일 *'Oppan Gangnam Style'* (Korean for *Oppa*, an older male friend, has *Gangnam*, from *Gangnam-gu* – the glitzy part of Seoul city centre – *style*)

Similarly, language learners will be familiar with a range of expressions from English songs, but may not yet have considered using these words in other contexts.

To start this activity, I have chosen the song *Blame It on the Boogie*, originally co-authored by Mick and David Jackson and Elmar Krohn, but most successfully performed by *The Jackson 5* (no relation to the songwriters).

The song should be an easy example to identify, allowing learners to move on to their own songs.

Setting up
Copy and cut out the strips opposite, so that there is one line for each learner:

■ It doesn't matter if several learners receive the same line.

Prepare a further five to eight blank cards for each learner to write on.

Step by step
■ Ask your class to think of a popular English language song that they perhaps like to sing along to:
  □ This can sometimes be an 'earworm' (a catchy song that repeats continually in their minds even when it is not playing).
  □ This song can be new song or an oldie, a rock or pop song, a festive carol or an anthem.

Don't blame it on the sunshine

Don't blame it on the moonlight

Don't blame it on good times

I've changed my life completely

And that's no lie

I've seen the lightning leave me

And my baby just can't take her eyes off me

A fire burns inside me

■ Give your learners the blank cards that you prepared, and ask them to try to write one line from their song on each.
  – If they struggle, ask them to search online for the lyrics.
  – To keep things simple, these lines should be no longer than about eight words.
  □ You might want to check with the learners – to see if the language is appropriate for your classroom – before continuing.
  □ Tell the learners to keep these lines secret from the rest of the class.

■ Tell the class that you would like them to try to use song lines in class conversation:
  □ Start with your example song.
  □ Ask for eight volunteers, and give each of them one line from *Blame It on the Boogie*.
  □ Tell these learners that you would like them to try to think of a context for their lines and to discreetly slip these into a conversation.

■ Start the conversation:
  □ As soon as the other learners think they recognise the song, they should tell the class.

■ Next, ask all the learners to try to include *their own* lines in a class conversation:
  □ As soon as a learner suspects another of using a line from a song, and recognises that song, they should tell the class.

Blame it on the boogie

- ☐ The objective is for the learners to use all their lines, as naturally, and unnoticeably, as possible
- ■ At the end of the lesson, ask the class to reflect on what everyone said:
  - ☐ *Can they remember what their classmates said?*
  - ☐ *Which of these things do they think might belong to a song?*
  - ☐ *Can they guess the song?*

Signing off

Research into language acquisition, such as that carried out by *The Journal of The Acoustical Society of America* and *The Journal of Memory and Language*, suggests that even passive listening to a language – such as listening to songs in the background – can enhance the learning of vocabulary and structures:
- ■ Song lyrics can also help learners understand syllable timing and recognise colloquial or non-standard forms of speech.

Encourage your learners to listen to an English language radio station in their free time – using, for example, *Radio.garden* or *MyTuner*, which are both available as websites and apps.

Adjacency pairs

Contextualised conversational 'turn taking'

Strategy
Understanding unexpected responses and ambiguity.

Setting the context
The ability to recognise ambiguity in conversation can mean 'make or break':
- ■ Not just in social interactions, but also in minimising any breakdown in communication when attending meetings or taking part in negotiations.

When asking someone the time, for example, I often used to say: *'Have you got the time on you?'*
- ■ One day, I stopped a stranger on the street, who replied: *'Yes I have, thanks'* – and walked off.
- ■ Since then, I have not used that phrase.

As we each take our turns to speak, we may receive alternative responses to those we had expected.

Such 'adjacency pairs' will depend on differing levels of 'distance' between the speakers – on intrusion, urgency, and, perhaps, on the sense of humour of the speaker and the hearer.

Setting up
Prepare a copy of the Table on page 55 for each learner.

Bring plenty of scissors!

Step by step
- ■ Write 'I love you' on the board, and ask the class:
  - ☐ *When might they say or hear these words?*
- ■ Explain that, besides showing affection, the same words can also be used:
  - – as an alternative to 'goodbye' – for example, when family members speak on the phone;
  - – as a 'softener'– before a request, or after an accusation;
  - – as a way of saying thank you – for a present or a gesture.
- ■ Ask the learners if they can think of any *other* contexts – in English, or in another language that they speak.
- ■ Tell them that, when we communicate, we take turns – and that the responses we give depend very much on the context in which they are said:
  - ☐ A good example of this is to do any 'mix and match' exercise from a coursebook, and discuss *alternative* answers to the one provided.

▶▶▶

Adjacency pairs

- Give each learner a copy of the Table, and give them a few minutes to fill out the first column by writing a response to the statement in each box. For example:
  - The expected response to a greeting – *'Hello'* – is another greeting: *'Good afternoon'*.
  - The expected response to a compliment – *'I really like your handwriting'* – is a thank you.

  Other *expected* responses are:
  - Question – answer
  - Request – acceptance/denial
  - Apology – forgiveness
  - Opinion – (dis)agreement.
  - Accusation – acceptance/denial
  - Offer – acceptance/denial
  - Assertion – acknowledgement/disagreement.
  - Instruction – compliance/refusal

- Go through the first column of the table together, and elicit some sample responses.

- Now ask the learners to complete the second column:
  - They should, this time, keep their responses hidden from the other members of the class.

- When they finish, ask them to cut out their responses from both columns into individual cards.

- Collect these in a pile.

- Redistribute the responses:
  - *How and when might the learners' phrases be used as unexpected responses?*

- Read out the statements in the first column once more.

- As you do so, the learners should call out the responses they think will fit:
  - *Can they also explain the context?*

Signing off

Ask the learners to look out for examples of unexpected responses from their own correspondence (eg emails or chat rooms) and, in a future lesson, to share these with the class.

	Expected response	Unexpected response
Hello! (greeting)		
Are you OK? (question)		
Sorry, have you got the time? (question/request)		
I'm sorry I'm late. (apology)		
I really like your handwriting. (compliment)		
I think the Earth is flat! (opinion)		
It's all your fault I got a bad grade! (accusation)		
Can I help you carry your books? (offer)		
The autumn is beautiful here. (assertion)		
Could you lend me £10? (request)		
If your computer is not working properly, restart it! (instruction)		

Windy lifts, *schody* stairs

Decontextualised messages from public notices and advertising

Strategy
Understanding the – mostly – written messages of advertising or public signs in the learners' urban surroundings: also known as the 'linguistic landscape'.

Setting the context
A seemingly inappropriate or clever use of the language that we see around us can often be a source of laughter.

There are photographs of funny examples of English, some of them either:
- questionable
  (eg a German hamburger chain – '*Burgerme*')
- accidental
  (eg a Swedish ad for a vacuum cleaner –
  '*Nothing sucks like an Electrolux*'),
- intentional
  (eg a drink driving campaign on an Arizona freeway –
  '*Drive hammered, get nailed*')
- confusing
  (eg on a door in Northern Spain '*Spanish Snail S.L.*')

Other times, the language may seem odd – but make perfect sense in *context*:
- In Poland, where the word for *lifts* is 'windy' and the word for *stairs* is 'schody', there is nothing unusual about these words appearing side by side in places frequented by international guests, such as in a hotel lobby.
- Out of context, however, the Polish words can appear to be adjectives (*windy*, *shoddy*) which describe the *English* word.

Setting up
In preparation for the class, photograph or collect examples of English from the learners' everyday surroundings, such as advertising, billboards, instruction manuals, etc – where the context or product are not immediately obvious:
- These can be real or 'accidental'.

Ask your learners to do the same, ideally using use their mobile devices, as a homework or holiday task.
They should bring these to the lesson.

Step by step
- Ask the learners to share with the class the photographs they took:
  - *Can they identify where the words came from, and what product or service they refer to?*
- Show the class your own examples of language from 'linguistic landscapes' (these can be local or from other areas, such as an English speaking country):
  - *Can the learners guess what the message is, and what it is trying to encourage people to do?*
- Ask the class:
  - *Which messages did they think were especially clever or original?*
  - *Which were accidental, questionable or confusing?*
  - *Can the message be translated – so that it will also work in their first language?*
  - *If not, why not?*

Signing off
Encourage your learners to keep up their records of English in *their* linguistic environment:
- You may also encourage them to come up with new English slogans or names of their own.

They might even like to share these in a Facebook group such as the *Map of the Urban Linguistic Landscape* (MULL).

Song lyrics roleplays

Understanding phrases from their contexts

Strategy
Recognising how the same phrases adopt alternative meanings in informal spoken language.

Setting the context
Roleplays can be good fun, but they can also limit the way language is used to a set context and a literal meaning.

Rather than giving your learners the context and asking them to assume roles that are perhaps unnatural, give your class the freedom to come up with the context *themselves*:
- This will help the learners to raise their awareness of how familiar phrases can be understood in different ways by the hearer.

This is the beauty, as well as the intrigue, of song lyrics.

Setting up
The word cloud below is made up of lines from popular songs by alternative English rock bands of the 1980s.

Make a copy of the word cloud for each learner, or prepare your own cue cards with individual lyrics from songs.

Step by step
- Give each learner a copy of the word cloud.
- Tell them that the lines come from popular songs from the 'Madchester' music scene (a cultural movement that originated in Manchester, UK, in the 1980s – with bands such as Joy Division, New Order, The Smiths, The Fall, Simply Red, etc):
  - Do they recognise any of them?
- Ask pairs of learners to select one line or phrase from the song and think about the different ways it could be used, besides the one that is immediately apparent:
  - Who is addressing who? Why?
  - Could 'I've lost you', for example, mean:
    – that the speaker can't find the hearer?
    – that a telephone or radio signal is too weak to hear what the other person is saying?
    – that the speaker is unable to understand what the other is saying?
- Ask the pairs to write a short dialogue including this phrase.
- When they have finished, the pairs read their dialogues to the rest of the class, who discuss the meaning and guess the context of the line chosen.

Signing off
The learners look at the lyrics of their favourite songs, and then check the meaning on websites such as:
– songmeanings.com
– songfacts.com

Roger Irrelevant

Recognising relevance and cognitive bias

Strategy
Recognising that words can have many different meanings.

Setting the context
The British comic magazine *Viz* features a character called Roger Irrelevant (*'He's Completely Hatstand'*), who continually gives irrelevant and surreal responses in conversation.

The following game of word association encourages the learners to use the words they know in a fun and inventive way, as well as to consider how they use a dictionary.

Setting up
None is necessary.

Step by step
- Write the word *bread* on the board.
- Ask the class to tell you which words they immediately associate with this word:
  - They may tell you:
    - *sandwich*;
    - *toast*;
    - *butter* …
- Explain that these may be immediately obvious, and could be given in the *first* entry of a dictionary.
- Ask the class to look up the word, and tell you alternative meanings of the word *bread*.
- Now ask them what *other* words they could have given to the ones they called out before:
  - For example:
    - *money*;
    - *wage*;
    - *carpenters* …
- Tell the class that they are going to play a word game: a word association game.
- Choose any common noun, perhaps vocabulary that has recently been described in class, and ask each learner to suggest words that come to mind:
  - If possible – but this is not essential – these should be words that are not immediately obvious.
  - If you find some especially clever, praise them.
  - If a learner gives a word you do not think *relevant*, ask them to explain the connections.
- When a word is not considered relevant, or if a learner fails to come up with a word, they are out of the game:
  - You mght like to make a note of the connections that you especially liked.
- The winner is the last learner to remain in the game.
- Together with the learners, reflect on the notes that you made and remind the class of the importance of not always choosing the first definition that they find in the dictionary or on an online translation site.

Signing off
Ask your learners which online dictionaries or translation tools they know:
- *Do they think that these are reliable?*
- *Can they think of any examples when, on a search for a word, they have been given surprising results?*

As a class, compile a list of favourite or most reliable online dictionaries to distribute to all the learners.

CHAPTER TWO • ENGLISH IN CONTEXT

Larkin' about

Deciphering meaning from context

Strategy
Rebuilding written texts and making sense of chaos.

Setting the context
The Telephone Game is a game where players pass on a message along a line by whispering it from one to another.

Getting your learners to pass on sentences or short phrases from a set text such as a poem can help them contemplate the theme and meaning of the poem, when they try to make sense of the complete piece.

Setting up
Select a short poem of about 10 lines.
Print a copy for each learner.

For this activity, I have chosen as an example *Days* by Philip Larkin, as the words and structures are simple, yet it is open to very different interpretations:
- Are the priest and the doctor actual people – or are they metaphors for religion and science, for example?
- Which one saves the day?

It is available online at *poetryfoundation.org*; as well as on *YouTube*.

Step by step
- Check with your learners that they are all familiar with The Telephone Game.
- Tell them that you have a number of sentences that you will whisper to them, and you would like them to pass them on around the class.
- Whisper the first line of the poem to a learner and ask them to repeat that same line by whispering it to the nearest person:
  - This continues until the message reaches the last learner in the class.
- While this is happening, engage the rest of the class in conversation – so that the learners who are not listening to the whispered message are distracted from trying to hear what the line is.
- When the last learner receives the message, ask that learner to write it on a board or flipchart that is not visible to the rest of the class.
- Now take the second line, and whisper it to a different learner from the one who started before.
- The class repeat the same steps, until the message reaches a different learner to the one who was last before:
  - This learner then writes the message beneath the first message on the concealed board.
- Once all the lines have been completed, show the class what they have written.
- Tell the learners that all the lines make up a single poem:
  - The chances are that their version will be very surreal, with only one or two lines similar to the original.
- Ask the class:
  - *What do they think the poem they have written could be about?*
  - *Who was the speaker?*
  - *How were they feeling?*
- Give the class a few minutes to suggest and 're-piece' what they think was in the original poem:
  - Help them by telling them that the words they have written on the board may either be the *same as*, or *sound like*, the original.
- Show the class the original poem, or play them an audio recording from *YouTube*:
  - *How similar is their version to the original?*
  - *What do the class think the poem is about?*
  - *Were the learners right about the topic and situation of the poem?*

Signing off
Ask the learners to share poems that they like by reading them aloud to the class.

If they can't think of a poem, ask them to begin searching by writing 'poem' in *Google Images*, and selecting a meme, jpg/jpeg, etc, and to choose one. Ask them to tell the class:
- *What does it mean to them?*
- *Why do they like it?*

Reference
Days by Philip Larkin
(From *The Whitsun Weddings*, Faber and Faber 1964)

CHAPTER TWO • ENGLISH IN CONTEXT

A word is a word – or is it?

The properties of words

Strategy
Contemplating what words express, and how they are used.

Setting the context
Besides their meanings, some words are also examples of what they describe:
- *unique* is the only word with that spelling to describe something of which there is only one;
- *unhyphenated* has indeed no hyphen;
- *real* and *regular* do exist, and are used regularly;
- *harmless* carries no prejudice or threat to inflict damage.

Words such as these are *autological* or *homological*.

Other words are *not* examples of themselves:
- *yellow* has no colour;
- the spelling of *old* (with no *e*) is relatively new;
- *verb*, as many teachers tell their learners, is 'a doing word' and, consequently, a noun;
- *wasp* does not actually fly around and threaten to sting you when you're enjoying an ice-cream on a hot summer's day.

These words are, therefore, *heterological*.

Thinking about words as homological or heterological (see also *Simile, please!* on page 86) may hardly seem exciting:
- But it can help your learners visualise, and subsequently memorise, words and their contexts.
- Perhaps the more these learners consider the qualities of such words, the more they will hunt!

Setting up
None is necessary.

Step by step
- Write the following words on the board:

    English   Spanish   readable   giraffe

- Tell your class that these words can be divided into two groups (they don't need to know the linguistic terms):
    - those words that are what they say they are (Group A).
    - those words that are not (Group B).

  English is an English word and we can read **readable**. **Spanish** is not a Spanish word, nor is **giraffe** a giraffe!

- Now ask your learners to create *three* columns on a sheet of paper, labelled: Group A, Group B – and Group C:
    - □ The words in Group C *depend* on the context.

- Dictate randomly (some of) the words in the box below:
    - □ *Can the learners put them in the appropriate columns?*

- Ask the class to compare their lists together:
    - □ *Can they tell you about differences in understanding?*

Signing off
Encourage the learners to continue their lists – perhaps by searching for autological words online, or by considering words they already know.

Group A
(autological/homological)

adjectival
(… it is an adjective)

meaningful
(… it has meaning)

common
(… it is commonly used)

single
(… it stands alone)

awkward
(… the spelling – two *ws* – is awkward)

Group B
(heterological)

relaxed
(… it does not relax)

cacti
(… it is not a member of the plant family)

hedge
(… it is neither a fence nor does it protect anything)

rainy
(… it is not even wet)

finance
(… the word may be a financial term, but it is not the management of money)

(… whether it is written clearly or unclearly)

Americanised
(… whether it is written with an 's' or a 'z')

forgettable
(… the individual's ability to remember it)

cool
(… whether the speaker considers it 'in' – or not)

iffy
(… the speaker's opinion of the word)

font
(… whether it is printed – or not)

pencil
(… whether it is written in pencil or pen, chalk, etc)

salad
(… whether the speaker considers it to be a salad of letters)

electronic
(… whether the word is typed or handwritten)

miniature
(… whether the word is written in tiny letters or not)

Group C (It depends …)

unclear

Felicitous conditions

The need for an appropriate context

Strategy
Understanding the seriousness or sincerity of what is said.

Setting the context
I call my dear friend James, a fellow country collector who I have known since childhood, 'Seamie'.

This is taken from *'Seamie's wi' us'* ('shame he's with us') – remember that *Seamie* is pronounced *Shame-y*):
- There's more about Seamie on pages 91 and 118.

Upon reaching the steps to the Royal Palace in Brussels, Seamie declared to everyone and no-one that:
- 'in the name of Prince Michael of Sealand', he hereby claimed Belgium as crown territory of the little-known nation in the North Sea.
- Using these words, he believed he was making an official claim. Perhaps not surprisingly, this 'speech act' failed.
- Nobody listened and nothing was seized, other than perhaps an arm.

To be able to effectively do things with words, certain requirements need to be met:
- The conditions must be favourable and appropriate for the context.

These conditions are known as *felicitous*:
- Seamie had neither the authority nor the ability (never mind the intention) to launch an invasion.
- Alone, cold, and perhaps more than a little bit merry, on the *Place des Palais* – the circumstances were hardly ideal for him to pose any threat to anyone, let alone the citizens of Belgium.

Setting up
Make a copy of the grid below for each group or pair.

Step by step
- Tell the class that the things we say will only be effective – or 'perform' effectively – if certain conditions are met.
- To illustrate the point, write the following on the board:

  'I plead the Fifth Amendment on that one.'

- Explain that the phrase could be used in an American court of law to say that you do not want to answer a question:
  - *How could the same phrase be used as a metaphor in a domestic setting, between partners or friends?*
  - *What effect do the learners think this would have on the hearer in such a situation?*
- Divide the class into pairs or groups and give each one a grid.
- Tell the learners that the phrase in each box performs an illocutionary function – or 'speech act' – which could be used:
  - in a *formal* situation, if the 'felicitous' conditions are met;
  - in an *informal* setting, where the sentence, perhaps with a change in intonation, appeals to humour, sarcasm or mockery.
- Check that the class all know the rules of the game of noughts and crosses, or tic-tac-toe.
- Explain that you would like them to play the game, using their grids.
- As a player chooses a box, they should explain which action or actions the line performs:
  - If the other players agree with the explanation provided, the player is allowed to enter a nought or a cross.

You are in so much trouble!	Please excuse my bad language.	I bet you a thousand pounds that he's innocent.
I wish you good luck with that!	I dare you to ask for more understanding.	I hate to disturb you while you're working.
Have you finished? Then I'll continue.	Welcome to the madhouse.	You must stop writing now.

Felicitous conditions

- If they disagree, or find the explanation dubious, the player does not claim the box, leaving it open for the opponents to claim.
- Once everybody has finished, go through each box with the class and ask the learners to share their situations.

Signing off
Ask the class to keep a running notebook of phrases they encounter – recording not just the meaning, but the situation in which it is used and what conditions are necessary for it to be effective.

Note:
Prince Michael of Sealand claims an abandoned platform 12 kilometres off the Suffolk coast, UK, as his territory.

He is taken a little more seriously than my friend Seamie. The two did once meet – but that's another story.

Visit the Sealand Government website to find out more:
https://www.sealandgov.org/

Soap bubbles
The definite article in context

Strategy
Predicting the context, topic and identity of speakers by looking at conversation starters.

Setting the context
In his book *Are You Listening?* Professor Ralph Nichols said:

'If you anticipate correctly, learning has been reinforced. If you anticipate incorrectly, you wonder why and this too helps to increase attention.'

In contrast to traditional coursebook dialogues, real-life conversations often start with a more 'unconventional' line than a greeting and an introduction to the topic.

By removing the first line of a conversation from its context, and asking learners to anticipate what is to come, we can help them understand how different scenarios are possible.

A wonderful source of such conversational starters, I find, is a long-running series, such as continuing soap operas (*Virgin River, Friends, Neighbours, Eastenders* …).

Setting up
Find out from your class which series they watch regularly and enjoy. Then search online (*YouTube* or streaming providers) for a recent episode of a series that is popular with your class, and write down the first lines of a conversation:

- Make sure the episode is still available when you have your class so that you can play the recording for your learners.

Alternatively, I have given a few examples at the end of the activity on page 63.

You could, instead, work with a recording from a *Cambridge Assessment English* listening test.

Step by step
- Ask the class about conversations they overhear when somebody is speaking on the phone, while on the bus or on the train.
- Tell the learners that, in these situations, they have no context and they can only guess what the speaker is speaking about.

CHAPTER TWO • ENGLISH IN CONTEXT

Soap bubbles

- Write your sample sentences on the board. For example:
  - 'Mr Fowler, are you OK back there? Do you need more air?'
    (Big Bang Theory, Series 11: Episode 24)
  - 'OK, so we know three kinds of verbs, which … took 40 minutes'
    (Community, S1: E24)
  - 'The new training session is tough. We just eat, drink and practise flying and that's hard work, isn't it?'
    (Test 3, Advanced 1, Cambridge English Language Assessment 2014)

- Ask the learners to guess answers to the following questions:
  - Who is speaking to whom?
  - Where are the speakers?
  - What are they speaking about?
  - What do any pronouns – such as 'it' in the last example above – refer to in the conversation?

- Elicit different answers from the class.

- Discuss the possible situations:
  - Which clues lead the learners to their answers?

- If you have a recording of the original episode, play the conversation to find out:
  - Who, if anyone, was closest to the context in the recording?

- Divide the class into groups of two or three.

- Tell the learners:
  - You will give them the examples of the starting line of other conversations (see opposite).
  - You would like the groups to discuss the situation together and then continue the conversation between the speakers, writing three or four more lines.

- When the groups have finished, ask them to read their conversations to the class.

- Play the original conversation, and ask the learners to compare this to their own understandings:
  - Did the groups miss any important clues?

Signing off

Tell the class about the world's longest-running drama series, *The Archers*:
- whose episodes first piloted on the BBC in 1950;
- whose episodes are available on *bbc.co.uk* as well as on *YouTube*;
- whose actors are often very similar to the speakers in the listening tests for Cambridge Assessment English exams, and may even be the same.

By listening to the series and getting used to the voices, it may help them prepare for these tests!

The examples below were collected from *Virgin River* (S1: E1), which follows the story of Melinda, a nurse who moves to start a new life in rural California.

Reference
Nichols, R G and Stevens, L A *Are You Listening?* McGraw Hill 1957

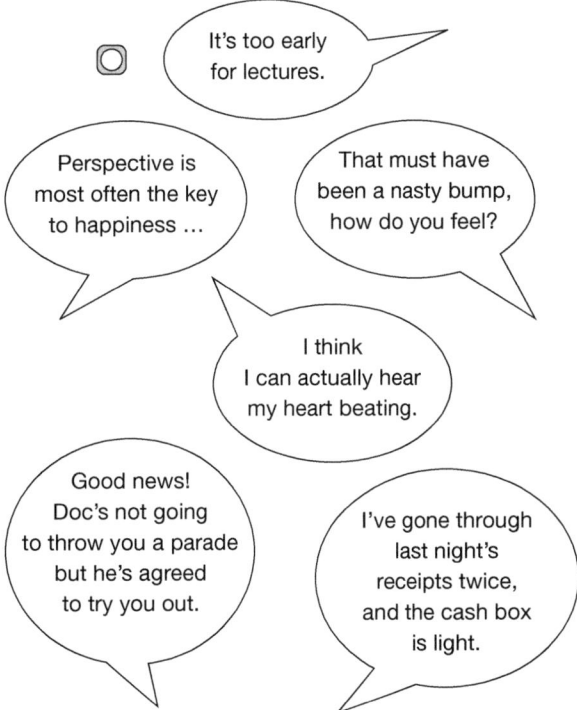

Simply apply dubbing

Providing language for an alternative context

Strategy
Considering alternative scenarios for a well-known film clip.

Setting the context
Whether it is ...
- a video clip of Laurel and Hardy in a restaurant or an interview with the Spanish comedian El Risitas (search *YouTube* for 'Laurel and Hardy restaurant' or 'El Risitas laugh') – all of whom are in an uncontrollable, and highly infectious, fit of laughter;
- or the fury of the Führer in the 'original bunker scene' from the German film *Der Untergang* (Downfall) ...

... these scenes – and others like them – have been parodied many times.

By providing new subtitles or dubbing to familiar films, *YouTubers* have successfully changed the dialogue from the original to a new one that perhaps gets the speakers to discuss:
- a disappointing sports result;
- the actions of a particular politician or celebrity;
- the fact that an outing originally planned to go to Lancashire will now go to Yorkshire instead.

These alternative versions have been so popular that they have quickly gone viral.

In *Song lyrics roleplays* (see page 57), we took individual chunks of language and created a context for them. Here, we do the opposite:
- The learners are given a scene from a famous film or video clip, and encouraged to create an alternative dialogue.

Setting up
Select a scene from a film or video involving two or more speakers:
- You can usually find these by searching on *YouTube*: 'name of film' + '??? scene'.

Scenes from films in languages not spoken by the learners are usually most effective, as the learners can still hear the voices and intonations:
- It is also, therefore, important that no subtitles are provided in the original film.

Step by step
- Show your learners the video clip, and ask them what they think it is about:
  - *Who are the characters, and what is the situation?*
  - *How do the characters feel about what is said?*
  - *What is being said?*
  - *Can the learners identify any words?*

- Divide the class into small groups, and ask each group to write a funny translation of the dialogue.

- When the groups have finished, ask them to:
  - play the video and simultaneously read their dialogue to the class;
  - alternatively, if the class are confident with video editing software, record their voices and add them to the clip.

- Ask the learners about their own experiences reading auto-generated subtitles, eg using algorithms to provide the dialogue through speech-recognition:
  - *How effective do the learners think these are?*
  - *How much do they rely upon them to understand what is said?*

When it comes to unusual pronunciation, or regional variation, these subtitles often fail – with hilarious results.

Signing off
Ask the class to find other parodies of the same clip online.

If your learners think that their version is better or equally funny, they could post their video in a *YouTube* group – and follow its progress.

Cannibalistic commas

How punctuation changes understanding

Strategy
Recognising the importance of punctuation, and its effect on the message.

Setting the context
Calling himself a 'grammar vigilante' and described by the press as the 'Banksy of punctuation', one infuriated resident of Bristol, England, sneaks out at night on a mission to correct 'poor grammar' in his home town.

Spotting mistakes on billboards, on shop fronts and on public notices, he feels compelled, for example:
- to add an apostrophe where one is missing;
- to remove another that should not be there.

While incorrect punctuation can be just wrong, at other times it can change the meaning of something completely – to the embarrassment of the writer.

Sometimes, these mistakes can have cannibalistic connotations!

Setting up
Prepare one 'station' containing one example of each sentence opposite, and print these. Put these up around your classroom.

Make sure you have enough marker or felt-tip pens so that there is one for each learner.

Step by step
- Write the following two sentences on the board:
  - I love cooking my dogs and my family.
  - I love cooking, my dogs and my family.
- Ask the class:
  - *How does the comma change the meaning?*
- Tell your learners about the 'grammar vigilante', or search for a video on *YouTube* to show them.
- Tell the class that you have put up examples of sentences that are misunderstood – due to poor punctuation.
- Tell the learners that you would like them to be grammar vigilantes, and give them each a marker pen:
  - They should walk around and read each sentence:
    - They can go around in any order they wish.
    - They should not all go to the same station.
  - They should use their pens to correct any mistakes.

- Let's eat George.
- Have you eaten Grandma?
- Enjoy. You're dinner!
- Best supper in town come and eat Father Mackenzie.
- Tables are for eating customers only.
- We're going to learn to cut and paste kids.
- I'm sorry I love you really.
- A panda eats, shoots, leaves.

- Once everybody has finished marking the sentences, ask them to sit down again.
- Go through each sentence with the class.

Signing off
Ask the class about the rules they know for using commas, full stops/periods, question marks and exclamation marks and ellipses:
- *Do you agree with what they tell you?*

In her book *The Pragmatics of Text Messaging: Making Meaning in Messages*, Professor Michelle A. McSweeney says:

'Many native English speakers have been told by many other native English speakers to "just read it aloud," and if the punctuation "sounds right", it probably is. This poor advice aside, this trend toward using more prosodic punctuation after many years of structural punctuation comes at a time when there is more writing than ever being produced for silent consumption (the text message, for example).'

The books below by Gyles Brandreth and Lynne Truss are particularly entertaining.

References
McSweeney, M A *The Pragmatics of Text Messaging: Making Meaning in Messages* Routledge 2018
Brandreth, G *Have You Eaten Grandma?* Simon & Schuster 2019
Truss, L *Eats, Shoots & Leaves: The Zero Tolerance Approach to Punctuation* Penguin Publishing Group 2004

An open book

Recognising different aspects of register

Strategy
Guessing the origin of a text and its genre, by considering the level of formality used by the speaker.

Setting the context
British linguists Michael Halliday and Ruqaiya Nasan described register as *'a variety of language, corresponding to a variety of situation'*.

In English, this is true, as the register we use depends on the purpose for which it is intended. For example:
- Who is the reader?
- Is the aim of the writer …
  – to entertain?
  – to inform?
  – to antagonise?
  – to appease?

In contrast to languages where formality depends on a choice of personal pronouns, English depends much more on *structure* and *lexis* to differentiate between usage.

Setting up
Collect one paragraph from four different kinds of books or printed material about a related topic that is relevant to your learners.

If the topic is *Scandinavia*, for example, these could be:
– a personal travelogue;
– a crime novel;
– a tourist guide;
– an academic paper on bronze age rock art …

Step by step
- Ask the class about the things they have read in English in the last few weeks:
  - What did they read?
  - Was this for business, or studies, or pleasure?
  - How interesting was the topic?
  - How motivated were they to read?
  - Would they consider the text to be written in a formal or informal style?
  - Why?
- Tell the learners that you would like them to read one paragraph from four different texts.
- As they do so, ask them to answer the following questions by making notes:
  - *What kind of text do they think each paragraph comes from?*
  - *What clues are provided?*
  - *Who do they think the intended audience is?*
  - *What is the writer's relationship to the reader? (eg close, distant, formal)*
  - *How does the writer describe the topic:*
    – positively?
    – negatively?
    – neutrally?
  - *Do the vocabulary and grammatical structures help your learners to answer these questions?*
- Once all learners have finished making notes, ask them to discuss their answers with the class:
  - *Which, if any, of the texts do they want to continue reading?*

Signing off
In his book *The Five Clocks*, Martin Joos identified five different aspects of register:
– *Frozen* (prayer, chants and poems)
– *Formal* (monologue and academia)
– *Consultative* (semi-formal discussion between different levels of hierarchy)
– *Casual* (informal exchanges between friends, slang and banter)
– *Intimate* (close family and friends, pillow talk, etc)

Tell your learners about these aspects:
- *What is the consequence on the hearer of changing from one aspect to another? (for example: using a formal register with a close friend)*

References
Halliday, M A K and Hasan, R *Language, Context, and Text: aspects of language in a social-semiotic perspective* Oxford University Press 1990

Joos, M *The Five Clocks* Harcourt, Brace & World 1967

Cumulus corpus

Creating your own corpus and looking at significance

Strategy
Deciphering the content of texts and the relevance of their words using word clouds.

Setting the context
Corpus linguistics depends on access to vast collections of text (eg the *Bank of English* or *International Corpus of English*, etc):
- Sometimes, these may involve registration, downloading or a possible subscription to corpora that are not always relevant to your learners' needs.

For class purposes, I find word-cloud or tag-cloud tools a more entertaining or immediate reference than corpora – for learners who may not be budding post-grads in applied linguistics … or at least, not yet!

Setting up
Prepare a word cloud for the text that you wish to work with. See our example below.
- You can either project this on the board or print individual copies for your learners.

There are several online tools that allow you to change the font, colour and shape:
- For this activity, we have used:
  - *wordclouds.com*
  - *wordart.com*

Step by step
- Tell your learners that you have selected an article for them to work with.
- Before you give it to them:
  - Tell the learners that you will show them a word cloud with the words the article contains.
  - Explain that the size of the words in the cloud reflects the number of times that word appears (ie the larger the word, the more regularly it appears in the text).
- Ask the learners to consider the words shown:
  - *What kind of text do they think it is?*
  - *Is the text formal or informal?*
  - *How are these words used in the context of the text?*
- Now give the class the article.
- Ask the learners to read it:
  - *How right were they in their answers to the questions?*
- Check these with the class.

Signing off
Ask the class to search online for examples of speeches or famous rhetoric and to create word clouds of their own:
- They can then print these off and put them up on the classroom wall in a class 'gallery of rhetoric'.

As other members of the class walk around, they can guess and discuss the meaning and source of the words.

Greta Thunberg's speech: UN Climate Action Summit 2019

(Created using *wordclouds.com*)

I see black for you

The connotations of words

Strategy
Understanding semantic change, according to the associations we make and the context they are used in.

Setting the context
The title of this activity is a direct translation of *'ich sehe schwarz für dich'*, a German expression of pessimism, meaning something like: *'Things look black for you'*.

- It has been printed on post-cards, etc, as a 'funny' example of *Denglish*, a dismissive term for the creeping use of anglicisms in German.
- Similar examples in other languages include *Spanglish* (Spanish), *Chinglish* (Chinese) and *Franglais* (French).

The literal meaning of many words we use has changed since they were first introduced:

- *naughty*, like many adjectives, simply added a 'y' to describe the quality of having 'naught' – or nothing – and had a sinister connotation.
- *silly*, from *seely*, originated from a noun meaning *luck* or *happiness*.
- *random*, in the last few decades, in informal speech, has become a synonym of *strange* or *odd*.

And the words *swell*, *sick*, *deadly*, *smart*, *cool*, *ace*, *fab*, *groovy* and *bad* have all come and gone out of fashion as ways to popularly express approval – as well as show your age!

These semantic changes happen because we continue to use the same words in new contexts, which create new emotional and environmental connotations. (We explore this more in *A royal bastard* on page 80.)

A good example of how the meaning of words changes – depending on our culture, belief and very personal associations – is the associations we make with *colour*, and how we use different colours in idioms and comparisons.

Setting up
None is necessary.

Step by step

- Tell your class that we make different associations with different colours – green, for example, is often associated with the nature, envy and illness, prosperity or paradise:
  - *Can the learners think of any examples in English?*
  - *Are there similar uses in their own languages?*
- What associations do they make with *other colours*, in English or other languages that they speak:
  - *Can they think of any idioms that use colours?*
  - black (often symbolises: power, evil – idioms: *to be in the black*; *to paint something black*)
  - red (often symbolises: love or affection, rage – idioms: *to roll out the red carpet*; *see red*)
  - blue (often symbolises: calm, melancholy – idioms: *feeling blue*; *once in a blue moon*)
  - white (often symbolises: innocence, fear – idioms: *a white lie*; *to see the whites of someone's eyes*)
  - yellow (often symbolises: optimism, cowardice – idioms: *the yellow brick road*; *yellow-bellied*)
- Tell the learners that, in a similar way to colours, other words carry positive, negative and neutral associations:
  - *The word 'different' can be used to avoid saying that something is strange or unorthodox.*
  - *It can also be used to withhold excitement about something exclusive or unique.*
- Ask the class to create a table with three columns:
  - They label the central column 'Neutral';
  - They label the column on the left 'Positive';
  - They label the column on the right 'Negative'.
- Read the following words to your class, who should list each word in the column where they think it belongs:
  terrific   smart   follow   caution   fantasy
  notorious   skinny   easy-going   childish   bizarre
- Ask the class to compare their tables, and discuss the contexts in which they would use the above words:
  - *Some of these words may be 'false friends' – with regard to other languages that your learners speak.*
- Discuss if you agree with their understandings.
- Finally, ask the learners to suggest positive, neutral or negative synonyms for these words, and write these up.

Signing off
Encourage your class to collect examples of the language used by sports teams, political parties, NGOs or other campaigners to persuade others to either *support* them or share their *opposition* to an adversary or issue.

Ask the learners to share their examples, and discuss:

- How is the language used more effective than alternative *synonyms*?

Chapter Three
Being direct
From me to you

There are times when there is a need to say exactly what we mean, as directly as we can.

The reasons for this can be many:
- Perhaps there is an imminent danger and there is simply no time to bother with diplomacy.
- Perhaps, as many of us do, we live in a culture where using pleasantries and making idle chat is considered 'dishonest', and using terms of endearment with strangers is highly uncomfortable.

With perhaps more than a bit of imagination, stripping our utterances of all this 'fuzzy language' can be compared to a cleanly shaven head! George Lakoff said *hedges* are 'words whose job is to make things fuzzier or less fuzzy'. (Lakoff, G 'Hedges: A Study in Meaning Criteria and the Logic of Fuzzy Concepts' *Journal of Philosophical Logic* 2 (4) Springer 1973.)

So we speak of being '**bald on record**'.

There are times when there may be a very good reason for such brevity – like giving clear instructions for how to make a face mask out of a pair of pants, or warning the captain of an ocean-going liner that there is an iceberg in the vicinity.

But we should not dismiss the idea that the speaker's aim may also be to make a personal attack – eg by 'heckling' (See *Here is the news* on page 70) or other affronts to the hearer's face – so we will see ways to defend ourselves when this is the case.

Here is the news

Heckling and responding to negative impoliteness

Strategy
Participating proactively and challenging ideas in an open discussion.

Setting the context
Interrupting public speakers with challenges and opinions need not always be aggressive. Provided the speaker is tough enough to interact with such 'hecklers', it can be entertaining for all concerned:
- In the language classroom, it can also be used as a way to involve everyone during a presentation – and provide support for the learners who need to defend themselves in discussions.

Heckling, which originally meant 'to comb out unwanted fibres from rope', came from the factories of Dickensian Britain. It was considered an exhausting test of tolerance, and those who managed to stick it out were considered to be capable enough to handle almost anything:
- As they worked, one person would be selected to entertain his/her colleagues by reading the day's news aloud.
- As the news was read, the workers interrupted, commented and started passionate debates.

Recreating this activity in your classroom will encourage the learners to contribute actively to debates.

Setting up
Collect examples (one for each learner) of news stories that you know will interest, or affect, your learners' lives:
- Choose wisely, with consideration of the learners' culture and beliefs.
- Traditionally, PARSNIP (Politics, Alcohol, Religion, Sex, Narcotics, -Isms, Pork) has been avoided in ELT – but *you* know *your* learners best.

Examples could include:
- A poor performance in a sports event;
- Industrial bad practice;
- Inappropriate behaviour of a celebrity or role model;
- A controversial film or book;
- A conspiracy theory.

No rope necessary!

Step by step
- Show your learners examples of hecklers – perhaps at Speakers' Corner (see the activity on page 71) – in stand-up comedy or in Parliament (such as *Prime Minister's Questions*).
- Discuss the approaches they used:
  - Were the attacks funny or impertinent?
  - Did they show support?
  - Or were they direct challenges?
- Ask each learner to pick a news item to read out loud to the rest of the class.
- As they do so, the others should participate, making as many comments as they can while they listen:
  - The speaker does not need to defend the story.
- After each story, ask the learners to repeat the language that they used to interrupt or contribute:
  - Did they hedge their sentences or apologise ('I'm sorry, but that's rubbish.')?
  - Did they perhaps use humour, in-group identity markers ('my friend', 'sister', 'mate' …)?
  - Were they indirect ('What have you been reading?')?

Signing off
Different newspapers, depending on their bias or readers, will report the same story in different ways.

Collect differing reports of the same story – perhaps with an obvious example of a 'conspiracy theory' – and, with the class, examine the focus of these stories:
- How do the writers attempt to appeal to the emotions of their readers?

Ask the learners:
- Which emotions is the writer is trying to achieve?
- How this is done?
- Which report connects with them most?
- Why?

Speakers' Corner

Handling face-threatening acts during debates

Strategy

Discussing, debating or handling verbal challenges during presentations. This can be useful for negotiators, customer service operators – or even budding teachers!

Setting the context

Speakers' Corner is a public area in London's Hyde Park, where anyone can speak, debate or discuss any topic of their choice:

- If the speaker is able to capture an audience, they may be rewarded by applause or cheers.
- They can equally be challenged with disapproval or counter-argument, which aim to discredit the speaker's knowledge of the subject – eg 'face-threatening acts' such as heckling or booing. (*Here is the news* on page 70 contains more information on 'heckling'.)

Learning to respond appropriately to such comments helps learners to improve their ability to discuss effectively, and to minimise the risk of being lost for words or struggling to find a suitable response – ultimately, it is a test of their linguistic stamina – and helps them to improve their fluency.

Setting up

None is necessary.

Step by step

- Tell your learners that you would like each of them to deliver a speech on a topic of their choice:
  - It is not important that they agree with the topic.
  - If they wish, they can play devil's advocate, but they should be ready to defend their argument.

  Some suggested topics could be:
  – Should mobile phones be allowed in class?
  – Is global warming exaggerated?
  – Are video games containing violence appropriate for children?
  – Can social networking sites do good?
  – Is peer pressure harmful or beneficial to individuals?
  – Is it unethical to eat horse meat?

  More topics can be found by searching online for 'debate topics'.

- Give the learners time to prepare their speeches.

- Once everyone is ready, write *(to) heckle* on the board, and explain that it can mean a mocking remark.

- Alternatively, go to *YouTube*: 'Speakers' Corner moments', and ask:
  - *How does what the learners see differ from presentations that they normally give in class?*

- Ask for volunteers to deliver their speeches:
  - Encourage the class to listen carefully and to feel free to comment, making sure …
    – they do so courteously;
    – they don't insult the speaker personally.

- Depending on the class, you may want to add some authenticity to your Speakers' Corner by providing a 'soap box' for the speakers to stand on.

- Reflect on the language and strategies used:
  – Empathy
  – Understanding
  – Witty response
  – Playful tease …

Signing off

Ask the learners to do an Internet search for advice on how to handle hecklers:

- A *YouTube* search, for example, for *Comedians* (such as Jimmy Carr) *vs Hecklers* will provide informative, and often very funny, suggestions.

Trollhunters

Recognising the language of aggravation

Strategy
Recognising aggressive utterances, and knowing what to do when such language occurs.

Setting the context
The Swedish reality TV show *Trolljägarna* (The Trollhunters) tracks down aggressive Internet offenders, and confronts them about the language they use.

By encouraging your class to recognise those whose sole aim is to antagonise or even hurt others online – and the language and methods they use to do this – you can help your learners to prevent such personal attacks happening to them or their friends.

Setting up
None is necessary.

Step by step
Ask the class to write a definition of an Internet 'troll'.

- Ask the learners to compare their definitions with the following examples:
  - 'A person who makes a deliberately offensive or provocative online post.' Oxford dictionaries
  - 'A person who provokes others (chiefly on the Internet) for their own personal amusement or to cause disruption.' Wiktionary
  - 'Internet troll – someone who posts inflammatory, extraneous, or off-topic messages in an online community, such as a forum, chat room or blog, with the primary intent of provoking readers into an emotional response or otherwise disrupting normal on-topic discussion.' YouTube

- Ask the learners:
  - Do they think trolls are always bad?
  - Do they think they can be healthy – depending on the context?
  - Do any of them admit to having ever trolled someone?
  - Where have they seen trolls?
    - Who or what was trolled?
    - How were the trolls dealt with?

- Ask them to find some examples:
  - What can they tell you about the language used by trolls?
  - Are there any typical characteristics that immediately alert them to their presence?

  Some suggestions could be that trolls:
  – use bad grammar, spelling and punctuation;
  – are abusive towards other members of a group;
  – don't give up!

- Explain that the best advice to deal with a troll is to ignore them, but it is often difficult to recognise one – until it is too late:
  - How do they think these responses could have 'fed' the trolls?

Signing off
Ask the learners to google 'Dr Claire Hardaker (Lancaster University)' and how to 'track trolls and cyberbullies':

- How do her findings compare to your learners' suggestions?
- Are there other ways that were not mentioned earlier by the class?

Ask the learners to read an example of a *Code of Conduct* from a website, blog or online games portal:

- Do they think that the platform deals sufficiently with the presence of trolling?

CHAPTER THREE • BEING DIRECT

Greta's world

Varying language to express urgency

Strategy
Reconsidering the modifiers we use in familiar terms and expressions – to add dramatic effect to, or to increase the urgency of, a familiar topic.

Setting the context
Journals and newspapers publish style guides to set a standard for the terms and expressions that they use to report their stories:
- Sometimes these stories are 'delicate' and require more tact or urgency than what the commonly associated terms or collocations suggest.
- At other times – such as when there is a crisis or impending threat – the publishers need to re-think the language they use, in order to describe the urgency of a situation.

The style guide of *The Guardian* newspaper, for example, has now stopped referring to 'climate change' – suggesting, instead, a climate 'crisis' or 'breakdown'.
- And the teenage 'activist' Greta Thunberg has become a 'warrior' for her cause.

Setting up
Collect a list of expressions, perhaps used by the learners themselves in a previous lesson – or used in their workplace, relating to a problem that they may be experiencing in their society or group.

Step by step
- Ask your class:
  - *What do they know about the problems faced by the environment?*
- Try to elicit the following expressions, and write them on the board:
  - global warming
  - biodiversity
  - fish stocks
  - climate change
  - climate sceptic
- Now, next to the words on the board, write the following:
  - global heating
  - wildlife
  - fish populations
  - climate crisis/breakdown/emergency
  - climate denier
    (*The Guardian* suggests that *denier* is more accurate than *sceptic*.)
- Ask the class what differences they notice between the two terms:
  - According to *The Guardian*, the second terms change the problem from being a *future* problem to one that is happening *now*.
- Tell the learners that you will give them a list of expressions that are commonly used.
- Give them the list that you collected when setting up the activity:
  - Terms used by people working in Human Resources, for example, could be:
    - behavioural competency
    - benchmarking
    - confidentiality agreement
    - emotional intelligence
    - gross misconduct
- Ask the learners:
  - *Can they come up with new expressions for greater impact?*
- Once they have come up with the new expressions, ask:
  - *Which do they think are excessive?*
  - *Which do they think are more effective?*

Signing off
Style guides can sometimes add more information about the context and appropriacy of words to a typical dictionary definition:
- They will, for example, tell us to use:
  - *care home* instead of *old people's home*;
  - *headteacher* instead of *headmaster* …
- And they will tell us why we should do so.

As a self-study task, encourage your learners to look for style guides of English language newspapers (*The Guardian*'s is free) and compare the language *given* to the language *they* would normally use.

They could then share their findings in a future lesson.

CHAPTER THREE • BEING DIRECT

Literally speaking

Pragmatic failure

Strategy
Recognising when and how messages are misunderstood – or fail completely.

Setting the context
A quick *Google Image* search for 'smartass-students' will deliver very funny, but at the same time clever, answers to typical school exam-type questions. For example:
- *'What is the difference between 'I have visited' and 'I visited'?'* …
  has the answer 'have'.
- *'What is the main reason for divorce?'* …
  gives the answer 'Marriage'.
- *'What state does the Kern River flow in?'* …
  provides the answer 'Liquid'.

Selecting a number of such questions – and then asking your learners the questions – makes for a fun way to practise alternative understandings and ambiguity.

Setting up
Select several questions to work with.

Step by step
- Tell your learners that you are going to give them a quiz, and that they need to think carefully about their answers:
  - See the questions opposite.
  - You may also like to use the examples above.
- Carry out the quiz, asking the learners to call out – rather than write down – their answers, so you can correct as you go:
  - For the first two questions above, they will struggle to find the answer they think you expect.
  - They will soon understand that you expect them to give *literal* answers.
- At the end of each question, explain the ambiguity:
  - How could the wording be changed so that there is no misunderstanding?
- Ask the learners to look for other similar questions on the Internet:
  - Which ones do they like the most?
- Ask them to share these with the class.

Signing off
Tell the class that misunderstandings such as those in the quiz – where there is a failure in communication or in understanding what is expected by the asker – could be an example of 'pragmatic failure' (eg mistaking a question or instruction for an invitation):
- It is perhaps due to an ambiguous word, lack of context, or uncertainty about whether a modifier belongs to the subject or the object of the clause.

When my own learners are working on something in class, and I ask *'How are you doing?'* – they often explain exactly *what* they are doing – they 'heard' *What are you doing?*:
- Similarly, the question *'Are you OK?'* is sometimes only expected when something is already wrong.

Ask your learners to tell the class any personal experiences of *pragmatic failure* – perhaps when visiting another country? – that they can remember or have heard about:
- *Was it a semantic problem or a cultural issue?*

- Draw four four-sided shapes (eg a square, a rectangle, a trapezoid and a kite) on the board. Ask the class to 'name the quadrilaterals'.
  Expected answer: *square*, *rectangle*, *trapezoid* and *kite*.
  Alternative answer: *Ronja*, *Bo*, *Sheila* and *Lou*.

- Show the class some Scandinavian flags, then ask the learners to draw the 'Finnish/Finish' flag.
  Expected answer: *A blue Nordic cross with a white background*.
  Alternative answer: *A chequered black and white flag*.

- Draw a right-angled triangle. Label the right angle and, next to each line, mark 4, 7 and X.
  Ask somebody to 'find X'.
  Expected answer: *8.083*.
  Alternative answer: *Here it is!*

- Ask the class: What looks like half an apple?
  Expected answer: *A semi-circle*.
  Alternative Answer: The other half.

- Ask: If you throw red paint into a blue sea, what will it become?
  Expected answer: *Pink*.
  Alternative answer: *Wet/a mess*.

CHAPTER THREE • BEING DIRECT

Clearing the dead wood

Unnecessary words or verbiage

Strategy
Recognising the (un)importance of words in meaning and understanding.

Setting the context
In language assessment, such as *Cambridge Assessment English* exams, learners are often given a restricted number of words in which to write essays, etc – to demonstrate their organisational skills:
- A problem I often find with my own learners is that they have written incomplete sentences, or they lack cohesion and end up saying something quite different to what they had intended.

To help our learners understand how removing the unnecessary words (the 'dead wood') – and restricting the words that they use, or changing the order in which they use them – can lead them to the risk of changing the meaning that they had intended.

Setting up
Here, I have chosen to work with the story of Elias the Thief, although any short story (maximum 200 words), article or report, will work:
- Ideally, it should have a good balance of adjectives, compound nouns and modifiers.
- You will find the story of Elias at the end of this activity on page 76.

The activity requires zero preparation – and is a lifesaver when having to come up with something on the spur of the moment!

Depending on the time you have available, and your lesson aims, you may wish to write the text on the board, telling the story as you do so:
- I find this an engaging task to check class comprehension and deal with new vocabulary.

To speed things up, however, you can project the text as a workable Word file.

Step by step
- Tell the class that you are going to tell them a story.
- Write your story on the board:
  - Once the text is complete, divide the learners into small groups (ideally of four or five).
- Tell them that you would like them to play a game to shorten the text as much as possible:
  - Each team will take a turn to remove *one word* at a time.
  - If a team removes one word and the sentence is still grammatically possible, they win a point.
- You can allow them to change the meaning as well as the punctuation.
  - Changing the meaning makes it more fun … students love it!
- As the learners play the game, they automatically consider:
  - the structures they have available;
  - which nouns are objects or subjects;
  - what agrees with what.
- Stop them, and remind them of the (task-based) learning process that is going on:
  - As they proofread the story, they are carefully considering the structures and context.
- The game can continue until there are very few words left, but you may want to set yourself a time limit.
- At the end of the game, discuss:
  - *Which words were the easiest to remove?* (probably adjectives, compound nouns and modifiers)
  - *Which words could be replaced with punctuation?* (phrases joined by *and*, for example)

Remind the learners that these elements are the *first things* to look for when considering reducing the size of their texts.

Signing off
Tell your class that website designers need to carefully choose three to four 'tag words' that describe the site content:
- To help the learners organise their writing, ask them to summarise paragraphs or texts by writing three or four tag words.
- Looking for North Americans in Hamburg, I once searched for the words 'North American Hamburg Society' – only to discover I had joined an American group dedicated to the raising and exhibiting of the Hamburg breed of chicken.

Clearing the dead wood

Elias the Thief

Elias the Thief was a man of good standing, who only turned to his life of crime after an accident made him lame and unable to run the family estate. He stole from the rich and gave to the poor.

Sounds familiar?

Unlike his Sherwood predecessor, however, he had no band of merry men, and had to hide out in a dingy cave in the Arctic woods of Sweden.

After one daring raid, retracing his footsteps across a frozen lake in a pair of ladies' shoes, he avoided capture.

But inevitably he was discovered in his hideout, cooking potato dumplings.

In a last stand of defiance, he hurled them as grenades.

His ammunition depleted, he was led away to prison where he died in 1860.

Time has embellished Elias' tale, but I prefer this tale of a benevolent outlaw to one of a tragic kleptomaniac, who stole clothes and embroidered cushions from landowners' wives, dumping his loot at the doors of unimpressed country folk.

Tomorrow is yesterday
Words that depend on their context

Strategy
Avoiding confusion by understanding the implicature (the implied meaning) of words, and knowing when more clarity is necessary.

Setting the context
The Irish are known for their 'gift of the gab':
- My personal favourite, from a postcard of *'The things the Irish say'*, is:
  – *Today is the tomorrow we worried about yesterday.*

It is not just inspirational – but, linguistically, it is playful!
- Despite the use of deixis (words which depend on the context in which they are used) – for example, *today*, *tomorrow* and *yesterday* – it depends on the hearer being able to understand what it means.

Setting up
Prepare copies of the sentences you are going to discuss, if you decide to hand them out.

Step by step
- Write the example sentences on page 77 on the board:
  □ Alternatively, you may prefer to hand them out.

- Ask the class to guess:
  □ *What is the situation?*
  □ *Who do the learners think the speakers are, in each case?*

- Tell the learners about words which depend on context, and that these can refer to time, place and people – or objects:
  □ In the first example:
    – *you* can be singular or plural;
    – *here* depends on the location of the speaker;
    – *last night* could be any time from 17.00 to 06.00 – depending on the time zone at a particular place in the world.

- Ask the learners to underline all the deictic words in the remaining sentences:
  □ *Can they decide what each word refers to?*
    – (Answers: *you, it, we, they, this, that, those, here, around, now, today, next Tuesday, the days/weather*)

Tomorrow is yesterday

- Discuss each sentence with the class, asking the learners to explain the deictic words:
  - *How does the date of 'next Tuesday' change – depending on the day when it is said?*
    - (eg if the sentence is said on a Monday or Wednesday evening)
  - *Can the meaning of the words be relevant for just one of the speakers?*
    - (eg if they are speaking on the phone – but in different parts of the world)

You should have seen the weather here last night.
You'll still hear examples of it around, though it's now quite old-fashioned.
Those were the days, my friend: we said they'd never end.
We'll look into those next Tuesday; today it's phrasal verbs.
Even after all that time, they just chatted about this and that.
Today is the tomorrow we worried about yesterday.

Signing off

The late DELTA author (*The Company Words Keep*) and brilliant friend, Paul Davis, suggested asking your learners to look for the most frequent words to appear in wordlists such as the British or American National Corpus, and to identify which of these are deictic.

You might ask your learners to prepare mini-presentations on a word of their choice for a future lesson:
- how it is used;
- how it can lead to misunderstandings.

Author's note:
I really like this reference to 'mañana', a deictic word if ever there was one – not just *morning* or *tomorrow*, but something much more:
- 'Sure, baby, mañana. It was always mañana. For the next few weeks that was all I heard – mañana, a lovely word and one that probably means heaven.'
Jack Kerouac

References
Davis, P and Kryszewska, H *The Company Words Keep* DELTA Publishing 2012
Kerouac, J *On The Road* An autobiographical novel written in 1951 and published in 1957 (Wikiquote)

Chapter Four
Being liked
Love me do

There is a very good reason for calling the strategy which concerns endearing the speaker to the hearer '**positive politeness**'.

It involves finding common ground between speakers, including and involving one another in our groups, paying compliments, showing interest, sympathising and establishing good rapport by using language to be generally … 'nice'!

This strategy is, after all, typically – but not exclusively – used by speakers who already know each other well and perhaps share a common membership of a group (eg culture) or passion (eg yarn bombing: covering public objects with knitting or crotchet).

The activities in this chapter involve the language that we use to endear us to others, and make them enjoy being in our company.

As far as your learners are concerned, this is also the strategy they are likely to encounter in informal contexts – strolling down the High Street in an English speaking environment, in a social media chat, or climbing the ranks in an Internet game.

On these occasions, it may not be enough for them to know how to *walk the walk* – they also need to *talk the talk*!

Claiming common ground

Finding and recognising group membership

Strategy
Identifying common characteristics, values or beliefs to build rapport and facilitate agreement.

Setting the context
Claiming 'common ground' refers to identifying things that we share with the people we meet:

- These could be:
  - a shared interest, concern, belief or wish;
  - coming from the same town or having gone to the same school;
  - having mutual friends, acquaintances or even family members;
  - a shared experience.

Conversation often becomes a game of searching for things we might share with the people we are speaking to:
- Once we do find something we share, it provides a solid footing for communication and breaks the ice.
- It leads us to a feeling of togetherness that facilitates negotiation, allows us to resolve any conflict, and even starts us on the path to becoming friends.

For this reason, I regularly use it in the first lesson of any course.

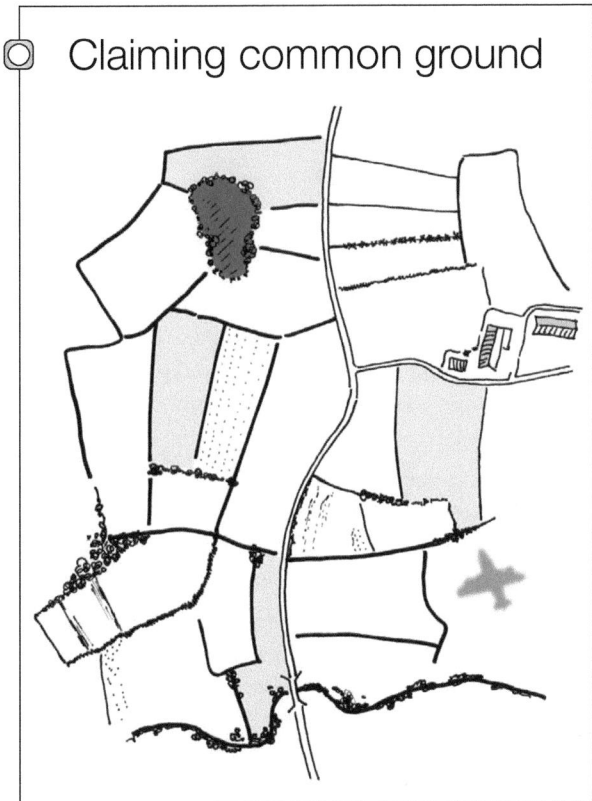

Setting up
Make a copy of the picture opposite as a handout for each learner.

Step by step
- Explain 'common ground', and ask the class for any personal examples/stories.
- Give each learner a copy of the handout.
- The learners write one or more words specifically about themselves in each field.
- You may need to ask a few questions to help them. For example:
  - *Where do you come from?*
  - *What music do you listen to when driving?*
  - *What are your hobbies?*
  - *What Internet games do you play?*
  - *What are you afraid of?*
  - *Have you met any famous people?*
- Vary the questions, according to the needs and aims of your learners.
- In pairs, the learners show their fields to one another:
  - They ask questions to find out more, and try to identify things that they have in common.
- Ask them to share with the class interesting facts they discovered about their partners.

Signing off
You may wish to make copies of the same handout for future lessons, to use as a familiar template for the learners to reflect on their course:
- to identify course aims/needs and perceived progress;
- as a way for you to collect feedback on your lessons.

A royal bastard

Using mock impoliteness to connect with others and build rapport

Strategy
Recognising non-serious conversation – such as banter and playful mockery – and what is acceptable in different situations.

Setting the context
In Ancient Greek mythology, the language of seduction, praise, encouragement and charm was personified in the nymph Eupheme:
- Today, her name survives in those 'nice' words that we use to speak about what we may consider awkward or unpleasant, instead of the words that everyone knows we shouldn't use – because they are too blunt or offensive.

But many of the words we adopt as euphemisms (*facility management*, *affirmative action*, *collateral damage*) eventually seem to plummet – in what we might compare to a bungee jump – to a derogatory and abusive low, only to bounce back to a new high … perhaps to fall once more.

One such example is the word 'bastard': it went from being a respected title of nobility to being regarded as an insult, but it may now be on its way back up:
- For example, when used among friends – as in 'you lucky bastard' – it is used as a term of endearment and respect.

Steven Pinker describes this transition of words, from the offensive to the acceptable – or even kind – and back again, as a 'euphemism treadmill':
- The words *idiot*, *moron* and *cretin* were once considered politically correct terms, but are now considered offensive.
- The word 'queer' was once used as a slur against homosexuals, but became an acceptable term:
  - with the LGBTQ community;
  - in academia (queer studies and queer theory);
  - in the arts (Fringe! Queer Film & Arts Fest).

Setting up
Make a copy of the image opposite to show to the class.

Step by step
- Show your learners the image, and ask them how they feel about it:
  - *Who do they think it speaks to?*
  - *Where does it come from?*
  - *Is it offensive?*
  - *Why does it use this language?*

Image derived from a popular sign in Australia to encourage people to eat more meat.

- Now explain that the word *bastard* has been used as a royal title, but then fell out of favour and was used as an offensive term:
  - Now, in some contexts, it can still be used as an affectionate term: for example, for someone who is extremely lucky.
- Ask the learners to think about other words they know are socially unacceptable, but which might be acceptable in some contexts:
  - *Can these words be used as in-group identity markers?*
  - *Do the learners know other words, which were once acceptable as euphemisms, but have now fallen out of favour?*

Signing off
English swear words are often used in L2 media as a 'cool' equivalent to their own L1 words – which sound much harsher.

Ask the learners to look for such examples and, in a future lesson, to explain how they have been used, and to what effect:
- *Can they give or find any examples of where offensive language has been used in advertising or media?*
- *How acceptable are these words, compared to their translations into the first language?*

Reference
Pinker, S *The Blank Slate: The Modern Denial of Human Nature* Penguin 2003

CHAPTER FOUR • BEING LIKED

Donald, Where's Your Troosers?

Identifying character from quotes and register

Strategy
Connecting with, and appealing to, group identity by identifying features of rhetoric.

Setting the context
The title of this activity refers to a comic Scottish song, which asks a kilt-wearing Donald where his trousers are:
- It was so popular that it made the UK music charts twice, 40 years apart.

Similarly, a popular urban myth claims that Donald Duck was once banned in Finland for not wearing any trousers:
- In his defence, you might argue that he does not need to wear clothes – he is, after all, a cartoon character!

This activity looks at well-known Donalds, but the 'trousers' in this case are the words of their rhetoric:
- The words that we use – in a similar way to the clothes we wear – reflect our personality.
- The context in which we use these words determines how (in)appropriate they are.

Setting up
Collect some sample sentences, quotes or lyrics – ideally, 20 to 30 words each – to work with in class:
- Your quotes can be from any celebrity, as long as the register is characteristic of that person.
- It is not important that the learners know all of them, as long as you give them some background information – so they can associate with the kind of person they are (job, culture, etc).

In the example here, I have chosen quotes by four famous Donalds:
– Duck (a cartoon character)
– Trump (the 45th President of the USA)
– Sutherland (a Canadian actor – his character here, from the film *Kelly's Heroes*, is Sgt. Oddball, a spaced-out tank commander)
– Knuth (a computer scientist and professor at Stanford University – called 'the father of algorithms')

Step by step
- Tell your learners that you have four quotes from four people – or characters – and give them the four names:
  □ *Does everyone know who they are?*
  □ *What are they famous for?*
- Give the class one quote at a time – without saying who is speaking.
- After each quote, ask the learners to guess who the speaker is.

> **Some suggested quotes:**
>
> 'Four dollars is very little money when you got 'em; but a heck of a lot of money when you ain't got 'em.'
> (Duck)
>
> 'People love me. And you know what? I've been very successful. Everybody loves me.'
> (Trump)
>
> 'Why don't you knock it off with them negative waves? Why don't you dig how beautiful it is out here? Why don't you say something righteous and hopeful for a change?'
> (Sutherland)
>
> 'The important thing, once you have enough to eat and a nice house, is what you can do for others, what you can contribute to the enterprise as a whole.'
> (Knuth)

- Reflect on the language used, and ask the learners:
  □ *What were the telltale signs when they made their guess?*

  – **Donald Duck** uses very informal language.
    (*'em, ain't*)
  – **Donald Trump** uses sweeping and often provocative statements.
    (*people love me, everybody loves me*)
  – **Donald Sutherland**'s character uses slang that reflects a group or era.
    (*negative waves, dig*)
  – **Donald Knuth** is neutral, factual, and uses longer words.
    (*contribute to the enterprise*)

Signing off
Ask your learners to find favourite quotes by other characters or celebrities that they know or like, and to share these:
- *Which words or expressions give the character of the speakers away?*
- *Have they adopted, or would they like to adopt, any of these expressions into their own everyday speech?*
- *Why (not)?*

It's no joke!

Using humour to build rapport

Strategy
Recognising appropriateness, and using politically correct language.

Setting the context
My friend Seamie (who you first met on page 61, and who also happens to be an engineer) was once advised that, to make sure his presentation to the company board of directors was successful, he should start with a joke:
- So when the next meeting came and it was his turn to speak, he stood up and began:
'There were two nuns in the bath …'

Humour can be tricky:
- It can be used to connect with, and also be liked by, your peers.
- At the same time, an ill choice of subject matter, or a lack of sensitivity to the hearer, can have the opposite effect.

This activity gets the learners to identify what can potentially cause offence, and how to put things more favourably in terms of political correctness – even if this means killing the joke.

Setting up
Prepare a copy of the example opposite – or another 'politically incorrect' joke – for each learner or group.

Step by step
- Ask your class for volunteers to translate a favourite joke into English, or share a favourite English joke:
  - *What do they think of the following types of humour?*
    - dirty
    - racist
    - black
    - sexist
    - sarcastic
    - sick
- Ask the learners if they think there is a time and a place for each of the above:
  - *Which do they think are offensive/not politically correct?*
- Tell the class that you would like them to rephrase a joke, making it politically *correct*.
  - Give them the example opposite, and ask them to underline any 'problem areas':
- Now ask them to re-write the joke. As they do so, they might consider the following:
  - Avoiding sweeping statements – adding *some/a few of the people* changes the acceptance of, for example, 'In Africa/China …'.
  - Using euphemisms:
    - replacing 'honest' with *keeping things above board*,
    - replacing 'opinion' with *conflicting viewpoints*, etc.
  - Adding 'hedging' devices (see page 106) – adding adverbs such as *sometimes/really/exactly* to 'didn't know'.
- Ask the learners to share their versions and reflect on the changes that they made:
  - *Do they think that they have killed the joke, or is it still funny?*
  - *Why/how?*

Signing off
Ask the learners to consider the jokes that they share with friends or that they like on social media:
- *Which of these are not appropriate, or could be taken wrongly outside of their 'circles'?*
- *Does this depend on the words used, or the topic in general?*

A worldwide survey was conducted by the United Nations. The only question asked was:

Would you please give your honest opinion about solutions to the food shortage in the rest of the world?

- In Africa, they didn't know what 'food' meant.
- In Eastern Europe, they didn't know what 'honest' meant.
- In Western Europe, they didn't know what 'shortage' meant.
- In China, they didn't know what 'opinion' meant.
- In the Middle East, they didn't know what 'solution' meant.
- In South America, they didn't know what 'please' meant.
- In the USA, they didn't know what 'the rest of the world' meant.

(The survey was a huge failure.)

The Ikea effect

Giving constructive and motivational criticism

Strategy
Using positive terms and expressions to suggest improvements, while motivating the hearer.

Setting the context
Professor Michael Norton of the Harvard Business School said that:

'Labor alone can be sufficient to induce greater liking for the fruits of one's labor: even constructing a standardized bureau, an arduous solitary task, can lead people to overvalue their (often poorly constructed) creations.'

In other words, whatever we do or make – no matter how poorly – we are biased in believing that our work is much better than it actually is:
- This cognitive bias is popularly called the 'Ikea effect'.

We may occasionally find ourselves in a situation where we need to give constructive criticism – while doing so positively, to avoid hurting the pride (and the possible 'threat to face') of the hearer.

Setting up
Depending on your learners' interests, do a *Google Images* search for anyone of the words below + 'fails': (eg cooking 'fails')

- art
- cooking
- DIY
- design architecture
- woodwork
- knitting
- engineering
- manufacturing
- sign
- drawing

Collect your favourite pictures, and add them to a *Powerpoint* presentation (one image per slide).

Step by step
- Ask the class to try to remember a time when someone tried to make something but didn't succeed – perhaps a child in their family brought home something they had made at school, or a friend who had attempted to do some DIY and was not successful:
  - *How did your learners respond?*
  - *Were the hearers motivated to try again?*
  - *Were they demotivated from trying again?*
- Encourage the learners to share their stories.

- Tell them that you will show them a selection of photos of attempts at making something that were not very successful:
  - *Can they call out any constructive criticism that they can think of?*

- Start the presentation, and write down the phrases that your learners contribute.

- At the end of the presentation, ask the learners which phrases they particularly like and which they think *they could use in the future*:
  - *Which of the phrases do they think will make the hearers like the speaker – ie the use of positive politeness strategies?*
    (See page 25.)
  - *Which will ensure that the hearers respect the speaker – ie the use of negative politeness strategies?*
    (See page 25.)
  - *Which phrases do the learners think are indirect and/or ambiguous and might be understood differently?*
    (See below.)

Signing off
Encourage your class to look for reviews of products or services that they regularly use, and to collect examples of feedback:
- *Can they find examples of comments that are ambiguous, or appear to mean the opposite?*
  For example:
  - Interesting concept …
  - One might question the logic …
  - You get what you pay for.
  - I'd like to have someone tell me what it is I'm missing here.
  - Great present for my mother-in-law.

This could be on a special interest website or a *YouTube* or TV programme – the British television series *Top Gear*, for example, is popular internationally for its entertaining reviews of cars.

Ask the learners to look out for expressions they particularly like, and to share these in a future lesson.

Age, sex, location?

Recognising identity through the language that we use

Strategy
Identifying with others, based on the language we choose to describe ourselves.

Setting the context
Subscribers to online friendship and dating sites often struggle with having to write about themselves:
- While wanting to tell others who they are, they also have to do so in a way that will appeal to the reader's interests.

Doing so – and going beyond the superficial 'a-s-l' (age, sex, location) question, which is often asked on first encounters in chat rooms – calls for the use of 'positive politeness' strategies: such as humour, group identity markers and slang.

Personal descriptions from websites such as *Tinder* and *Bumble* can help your learners recognise clues to who the author is, at the same time as perhaps identifying group membership or mutual interests.

Setting up
Copy each of the examples on page 85.

These examples are all inspired by entries on popular dating websites (*Tinder*, *Bumble*, *Parship*, etc).

Put each one onto a separate sheet of paper, and post them up on the walls around the classroom.

Step by step
- Ask your class if they know anything about dating websites:
  - *Do the learners have any experience of having used such a site, or do they know someone that has?*
  - *Was the experience positive or negative?*
- Tell the learners that dating sites require that you write a few lines to introduce yourself:
  - *What information do they think is important?*
  - *What do they think should not be included?*

  Tinder, for example, suggests that:
  - you try to engage with the reader, but try to avoid being unintentionally obnoxious;
  - you try not to be dull, but also not go overboard;
  - you don't think too much!
- Point to the personal biographies around the room.
- Ask the learners to get up, walk around and read the entries:
  - *Which do they like?*
  - *Which don't they like?*
  - *Who do they think the writers are (a-s-l)?*
  - *What do they find funny?*
  - *Is anything 'over the top'?*
  - *Is anything obnoxious?*
- Once everybody has read all the entries, ask for their feedback:
  - *Which 'bio' is the most/least popular?*
- Bearing in mind the things that the learners have read and discussed, ask them to write an introduction to *themselves*.

Signing off
Write the following question on the board:

How much does the language we use shape, and reveal, our identity?

Ask the class to debate the question, and to make a note of their answers.

The question comes from the article 'How Much Does The Language We Speak Shape Our Identity?' by Sheila Kohler, on *psychologytoday.com* (Nov 21, 2014).

Ask the learners to read this, or a similar article, and to compare it with their notes from the debate.

Age, sex, location?

'Truly an incredible person' Daily Times

'You'd be crazy to ignore this one' The Sun

'My hero' Wonder Woman

'My phone's background' My mum

'Sooo intelligent' My dog

Arcu

I have ants in my pants! If I don't get out of the house at least once a day, it drives me crazy. That's why I crave adventures – climbing mountains, canoeing or just going for a run in the forest. I'm also a sucker for strong coffee and love my sweets. Maybe you can be one of them. :)

Tilly

Assistant manager at McDonalds on my third shift. Favourite sport binge-watching sitcoms. Get along very well with black people. Look good basking in the sun, look better in dark corners at parties. Love the beach. Favourite food is jelly babies. I need u to send me a message telling me I'm beautiful.

KoJo

When I was 5 years old, my mother told me happiness was the key to life. When I went to school, they asked me what I wanted to be when I grew up. I wrote down happiness. They told me I didn't understand the assignment. I told them they didn't understand life.

Boring people, swipe left.

Lindsay

Sometimes I feel like I'm amature everythink. I cook, play the gutar, have 153 Youtube followers on my fashion channel, and look to try new things and learn new things. But I never really master anythink. I like to think that makes me different, if you don't like it, that's ur problem.

Soma

Shiny things distract me, people-watching is my favorite hobby. I live for those moments that you can't put into words – what could be better than share a good coffee with the people you love to be with most. On the weekends you can usually find me having a barbecue with friends, enjoying a beer while listening to the best music, but come Sunday and I'll be out exercising with my dog and getting ready for the week to come.

Fuse Silly

You want to know something about me? I'm that person who smiles and says hi to you if we are strangers passing on the street. I believe in kindness, empathy, holding doors open, putting your phone away at dinner, and always making time to listen to a friend. Oh yeah, and then there's the horror movies – the really, really bad ones. Guts. Gore. All of it. If you've ever heard of Suspiria, please message me right now – we need to talk.

Gulim

Lately I've been really into Paulo Coelho novels. I read The Alchemist when I was in college but I'm excited to find that his other stuff is amazing too. If you have any book recommendations, send them my way. I'm such a bookworm and love talking books. Currently, I'm doing a master's in education and live in the city, which I love. Live music is one of my other weaknesses. I'll see just about anyone – no matter how bad.

Dandelion

Simile, please!

Using alternative comparisons to avoid clichés and add emphasis

Strategy
Using and creating similes that are both personal and original, for greater impact on the hearer.

Setting the context
Getting learners to recognise clichés and come up with their own ways to compare things will not only help them improve their creative writing, it can also help them become entertaining participants in social situations – depending, of course, on the comparisons they make.

Setting up
None is necessary.

Step by step
- Write the following on the board:

  large   wise   entertaining

  Tell your class that these are adjectives – and ask for more examples.
- Write seven of their examples on the board.
- Now add the following:
  - as large as life
  - as wise as an owl
  - as entertaining as a clown

  Explain that these all use an *'as … as …'* structure, to make a conversation or piece of writing more descriptive than using the adjective alone.
- Now tell the class that the examples are rather boring – they are either clichés or lack originality:
  - You might argue that a clown is not particularly entertaining!
  - You are sure the class can come up with better comparisons.
- Remove the second part of the structures on the board, and replace them with the following:
  - as large as Liechtenstein
    (Thanks to my learner Farman for this.)
  - as wise as the fool who figured out that ignorance is bliss
  - as exciting as a 'behind the scenes' of a sloth's life
- Ask your learners:
  - What effect do they think these comparisons have on the hearer/reader?
- Explain:
  - While the first examples were obvious, these second ones probably have more impact – they are funny, sarcastic, or are visually more powerful.
- Tell the learners that 'as large as Liechtenstein' is especially clever, as it contains words which begin with the same letter (alliteration).
- Divide the class into small groups and give them some blank cards, with a different colour for each group.
- Ask them to work together to try to find effective comparisons for as many of the remaining seven adjectives on the board as they can:
  - As they come up with a comparison, they should write an example sentence on a piece of card, then hand it to you.
  - They do not have to do them in any order – they can choose any from the list.
  - Set them a time limit of five minutes to do this.
- At the end of the five minutes, read the sentences to the class and award points, according to the level of originality:
  - Which comparisons raise the most laughs?
  - Which sound like clichés?
  - Which make good sense?
  - Do any of their examples alliterate?
- Finally, ask the learners:
  - Which do they think they might adopt in the future?

Signing off
Tell your learners that the comparisons we make (similes, metaphors, etc) often reflect the character, interests or profession of the speaker:

- *Did the comparisons they came up with give any clues to the learners' character or interests?*
  - as useful as an old drill bit
    (from someone who likes DIY)
  - as good as something my five-year-old child could draw
    (about someone who is not very artistic) …
- *How easy would it be for someone from a different background to identify with the comparisons?*

Celebrity agony aunts – and uncles

Expressing engagement and sympathy

Strategy
Using language to demonstrate active listening, and exploring ways to express empathy with the speaker.

Setting the context
Newspapers, webzines and journals often feature an 'advice column', where readers are invited to send in letters to explain a problem.

Usually, these letters will be addressed to an expert, asking for advice in their field:
- love
- relationships
- health (typically, a doctor)
- consumer advice
- common interest or hobby
- working conditions
- cultural differences …

These experts are popularly known as 'agony aunts'.

The columns can be serious, but are also often frivolous and can make fun of a predicament:
- *The Sunday Times Online* and *Rolling Stone Magazine*'s Agony 'Uncle', for example, is Dr Ozzy Osbourne – who has, in his own words: *'survived drug addiction and dysfunctional family life, and is now solving your problems via social media.'*

Setting up
Either search online for a 'problems page' or 'personal problems solved', and collect some examples of letters to agony aunts/uncles that you know your learners can associate with.

Alternatively, use one of the two examples on page 88.

Print one copy of your example for the class.

Step by step
- Ask for a volunteer to read the problems that you have selected.
- Tell your class that you would like them to show the reader that they are listening – by expressing their sympathy. Examples could be:
  - *No, really? That's terrible.*
  - *Such a shame.*
  - *I'd do the same.*
  - *I know what you mean.*
  - *Tell me more.*
  - *Poor you!*
- Tell the class that the responses they gave were personal and typical of friends speaking to one another:
  - *How might they respond in other contexts?* (You write down the examples that they give.)
  - *How would the register change if the situation was more formal, such as:*
    - *when speaking to their boss or an elderly relative?*
    - *when writing business letters?*

Remind the class that the more formal the situation, the more distancing is expected:
- use of plural pronouns – *we* instead of *I*;
- turning verb phrases into noun phrases ('nominalisation' – see page 103).

For example:
- *That's terrible.* (informal)
- *I'm sorry to hear that.* (neutral)
- *It is with regret …* (formal)

- *Poor you!* (informal)
- *I sympathise.* (neutral)
- *We would like to express our sympathy.* (formal)

- Divide the class into small groups and ask them to think about the rhetoric of a famous person from history, a celebrity, or a fictional character that they would instantly recognise.

- To help them:
  - Ask them to briefly search online for their person's quotes, speeches and catchphrases:
    - Barrack Obama: *'Yes we can'*;
    - Robert De Niro: *'You talkin' to me?'*;
    - Sherlock Holmes: *'Elementary, my dear Watson'*.
  - Ask them to try to write a reply to the problem that was read earlier – using the typical phrases, and in the character of the person they selected.

- Once everyone has finished, ask the groups to read out their replies to the class:
  - *Can the learners guess who the celebrity is?*

Celebrity agony aunts – and uncles

Problem 1

I have a real problem, I don't know what to do.

It's my parents.

Every morning when I am trying to get ready for school, my mum makes me take the rubbish out. And then when I get home, the first thing she asks is if I've got any homework. She won't give me a break.

My dad is no better. When I finish my dinner, he tells me to go and do the washing up. I feel as though they're ganging up on me.

Then there's my little brother. He's such a pain in the neck. I love him but, whenever I finally do have time to myself, he wants to play football. I just want some 'me' time.

What should I do?

Problem 2

I don't know what to do.

I always look forward to my best friend coming to visit me in the summertime, but he can be such a pain. We have been friends since we were ten, but now we live in different countries and don't see each other as much as we would like to.

It is not a question of not having the money to visit each other, but because we both have very demanding jobs, our visits are restricted by time and we have to make the most of what we have. When we meet, it's like we saw each other yesterday, but that also means that it's not long until we start arguing!

My friend, for example, lives deep inland and I live on the coast. When he comes to visit, we always go to the seaside and that's when the arguing begins – because he always throws rubbish on the beach. He's the worst litterbug I know!

I have tried to tell him this, but then he says I'm an idiot and complains about poor public services, such as rubbish collection, where I live and insults my home. He gets angry and points at all the other rubbish, saying 'it will hardly make any difference, will it?'.

I don't want to fight when we have so little time together. I'm now afraid that, if we argue, maybe he won't come back.

What do you think?

Signing off

Ask your learners to look online for examples of Ozzy Osbourne's advice columns, or from a column in their own language:

- *How – if at all, and besides the language used – does the way of showing sympathy differ from typical examples in English?*

The word 'sorry' in English, for example, can be used in different contexts:

- In other languages, however, where the word for *apologising* is different for the word *to excuse yourself*, it often does not work in this context.

Reference

The Times: *https://www.thetimes.co.uk/article/dr-ozzy-osbournes-twitter-surgery-80vwks6l7w9*

Reports are from Mars, rapport is from Venus

How punctuation changes understanding

Strategy

Reporting facts or establishing intimacy.

Setting the context

The words 'report' and 'rapport' both originate from the Latin 'portare' – meaning *to carry*.

But while *reporting* involves explaining what has happened – carrying the story forward – having a good *rapport* means being in harmony with one another: 'carrying' the hearer.

This difference was demonstrated by American academic and professor of linguistics Deborah Tannen to explain how men and women converse:

- Men aim to achieve higher *authority*, by demonstrating their knowledge and correct opinion – eg when discussing politics, history or economics – and by giving the facts.
- Women try to *connect* with their conversational partners.

Setting up

Prepare a copy of the cards opposite so that equal numbers of learners can have either A or B.

Divide the class into groups.

Step by step

- Ask the groups to tell each other about a film or series that they have seen, or a book that they have read and enjoyed.
- Tell them:
  - ☐ You would like them to write about the story, based purely on what they can remember.
  - ☐ You will give them all a card with further instructions.
- Give each learner one of the two cards below (A or B):
  - ☐ They should not show their cards to one another.
  - ☐ They should write their descriptions.
- Once everybody has finished, ask the learners who had card A to exchange their stories with those who had card B.
- Ask them to read each others' accounts:
  - ☐ *What are the differences from what they wrote?*
  - ☐ *What effect does what they read have upon the reader?*
  - ☐ *What do they think were the instructions on their partner's card?*

A

Write an account of the story, explaining when and where it was set.

Who were the main characters, and what did they do?

Tell the reader what you know about the situation portrayed.

B

Write a review of the story, explaining why you liked it.

Would you recommend it to the reader of your review? Why?

Who were the main characters in the story? How do you think your reader would feel about them?

- Introduce the learners to the idea that different cultures have different traits:
  - from preferring 'masculine' traits of directness, assertiveness and facts;
  - to preferring 'feminine' traits of cooperation, modesty and empathy;
  - or vice versa.
- Write on the board:

  Cross-cultural communication

- Ask the class how the instructions on card A and B reflect this.
- Above the words on the board, add:

  Male–female conversation is …

- Tell the class:
  - ☐ For most women, the language of conversation is primarily a language of *rapport* – a way of establishing connections and negotiating relationships.

Reports are from Mars …

- For men, conversation becomes more a case of *reporting* facts and events as they happened – and removing the emotional aspects or personal feelings about a subject.
- Tell the learners about Professor Tannen's book – the majority of the research was done in the 1990s:
  - *Do they agree that this is a fair reflection of how men and women communicate?*
  - *Do they think things may have changed?*
  - *How fair do they think it is to think of cultures as having the masculine and feminine traits referred to here?*

Signing off
A trainee teacher – Milly, who also works as a customer service operative in several languages – says that, besides switching her language or 'code', depending on who she is speaking to, she also switches her *character* in order to connect with the culture of her conversational partner:
- *Do your learners think they adapt their character according to the culture of the languages they speak?*
- *What do they think are the traits of the English language?*

Reference
Tannen, D *You Just Don't Understand: Women and Men in Conversation* HarperCollins 1990

Flattery will get you …
Distinguishing the genuine from the false

Strategy
Recognising the differences between *genuine approval* or *appreciation* (eg compliments and praise) and *flattery* – and the consequences of each.

Setting the context
Flattery may be well-intentioned, and is used regularly – depending on who the speaker is addressing.

Said to be the food of fools, flattery can be a valuable tool to 'butter someone up' and help you get what you want, but – if it is insincere or misplaced – it can lead to an unexpected rebuke and make you fall flat on your metaphorical face.

Setting up
None is necessary.

Step by step
- As a warm-up at the beginning of a lesson, ask the learners to either praise or pay a compliment to the people sitting next to or near them – within a space of, say, five minutes:
  - This can be for:
    - the way someone is dressed;
    - how well they did something in a previous lesson;
    - how they helped someone;
    - their good pronunciation …
  - As they receive the praise, they should also respond with what they consider to be appropriate.
- Ask the learners about the comments they received:
  - *Which did they think were genuine?*
  - *Which did they think were false?*
  - *Why?*
  - *How could they tell?*
- Write the comments on the board:
  - *What responses did the flatterers get to their comments?*
  - *Were they appreciated?*
  - *Why do the learners think they got the reactions or responses they did?*
  - *Were these tense and defensive, or were they calm and non-threatening?*
- Go through the answers together, and create two columns on the board:

Flattery will get you …

- ☐ Write the successful compliments in the first column.
- ☐ Write the unsuccessful compliments in the second.
- ■ Leave these on the board to help your learners consider the difference between the two.
- ■ Now, next to the columns, write the following on the board:

Praise fosters trust; flattery fosters mistrust.

- ■ Ask the learners:
  - ☐ *Do they think they are good judges of what is sincere and insincere?*
- ■ Ask the class to suggest more sentences that distinguish between the genuine and the false.
  Some examples could be:
  – Praise is appreciation; flattery is lip-service.
  – Praise asks for nothing in return; flattery has ulterior motives.
  – Praise aims to encourage; flattery aims to deceive.
- ■ Go through the two columns on the board:
  - ☐ *Why were the compliments successful or unsuccessful?*
- ■ Ask your learners how they speak to their closest friends:
  - ☐ *Do they feel comfortable paying them compliments?*
  - ☐ *Do they disguise these with indirectness?*
- ■ To round off, ask them:
  - ☐ *Do they feel they pay too many compliments? Or are they a bit too economical when it comes to praising others?*
  - ☐ *Would they themselves appreciate more praise for the work that they do? Or is this not important to them?*

Signing off

In a culture where compliments are not readily paid, speakers may disguise being complimentary and building rapport with what, to others, may seem an impolite assertion about the hearer (such as calling your father your *old man*) or making fun of an innocent third party.

My example (as this is what I know best), male friends in the South of England, may be uncomfortable with showing affection and, instead, make fun of one another by adopting alternative names that appear impolite:

- ■ I call my friend James (who you first met on page 61 and who I have known since childhood) *Seamie* – taken from '*Seamie's wi' us*' (Shame he's with us).

Examples

– 'Oh, Edmund. I do love it when you get cross. Sometimes I think about having you executed, just to see the expression on your face.'
Queenie, *Blackadder*

– 'Who has the brain of a Brussels sprout?'
Anne Robinson, *The Weakest Link*

– 'I don't think he could have done better if he'd heard what he was playing, in my opinion.'
David Brent on Beethoven, *The Office*

– Dear old granddad, bless him. He was about as useful as a pair of sunglasses on a bloke with one ear.'
Del Boy Trotter, *Only Fools and Horses*

- ■ James doesn't mind – in fact, he takes great pleasure in reminding me to do so.

In a culture where such 'mock impoliteness' or 'jocular mockery' is foreign, this may either be misunderstood or simply not understood at all – and perhaps lead many to remark they 'don't understand English humour'.

Many popular comedy sitcoms owe their success to such 'banter':
– *The Office* (remade in many countries);
– *Bottom* and *Blackadder*;
– *The Weakest Link* (also remade in many countries).

See the examples above.

Ask your learners about the series they watch, and to share their favourite put-downs from them:
- ■ *What is the effect of these on the hearers?*
- ■ *Are any of them really 'compliments in disguise' (ie mock impoliteness)?*

The Shakespeare hop

Identifying cultural and linguistic traits

Strategy
Being able to distinguish between the context and background of Shakespeare and hip-hop.

Setting the context
Akala is a British rapper, author, activist and poet. Calling himself 'The Black Shakespeare', he founded *The Hip-hop Shakespeare Company* ('THSC'), who describe themselves as – 'exploring the social, cultural and linguistic parallels between the works of William Shakespeare and that of modern day hip-hop artists'.

In the recording of his 2011 TEDx talk in Aldeburgh, UK, Akala challenges the audience to a quiz – to see if they are able to tell:
- which quotes come from Shakespeare?
- which come from a selection of different hip-hop artists?

Setting up
Select five or six lines from any two distinct writers or genres of your choice.

As the works of Shakespeare and hip-hop would at first seem very distinct – both in language and era – I have chosen Akala's TEDx Aldeburgh talk for my examples (see opposite).

Step by step
- Ask the class what they know about the two writers that you have selected:
  - *Which works do they typically associate with these writers?*
  - *Do they like or dislike the writer? Why?*
  - *What do they know about the writer's life?*
  - *Is there evidence of this in their work?*
- Tell the learners that you would like them to guess who wrote what.
- Show them one quote at a time:
  - *Which is hip-hop and which is Shakespeare?*
- After guessing the origin of each quote, ask the class to tell you why they think so:
  - *Does the subject give anything away?*
  - *Do the words sound modern or archaic?*
  - *Do they in some other way reflect what they know about the author?*
- Tell them the answers.
- At the end of the quiz, ask the class to share any observations that they made of the language used.

Signing off
Encourage the learners to look for clues as to how language is used to reflect social and cultural issues in the books or songs that they enjoy.

Reference
Hip-Hop & Shakespeare? Akala at TEDx, Aldeburgh, Dec 2011
https://www.youtube.com/watch?v=DSbtkLA3GrY&t=47s

 Quotes

i) 'To destroy the beauty from which one came.'
ii) 'Maybe it's hatred I spew, maybe it's food for the spirit.'
iii) 'Men would rather use their broken weapons than their bare hands.'
iv) 'I was not born under a rhyming planet.'
v) 'The most benevolent king communicates through your dreams.'
vi) 'Socrates, philosophies and hypotheses can't define.'

Answers

i) *Can I live?* – Jay-Z
ii) *Renegade* – Eminem & Jay-Z
iii) *Othello* – Shakespeare
iv) *Much Ado About Nothing* – Shakespeare
v) *Impossible* – Wu-Tang Clan*
vi) *Triumph* – Wu-Tang Clan*
* 'Wu-Tang Clan is an American hip-hop group and collective formed in the New York City borough of Staten Island in 1992' – *Wikipedia*.

The heckle therapist

Expressing sympathy to counter impoliteness

Strategy

Responding with sympathy, to diffuse or make light of a situation.

Setting the context

Picture the scene …

Someone says something witty or makes fun of you in the presence of others at a party:

- Try as you might, you just can't come up with an appropriate response.
- Then, as you leave, at the bottom of the staircase and about to leave the house, it hits you!
- You come up with the perfect comeback – but it's much too late, so you kick yourself for not having thought of it earlier.

The French call this predicament *avoir l'esprit d'escalier* – or 'staircase wit'!

One way to counter this, and have a lot of fun in the process – as the comedian Jerry Seinfeld discovered – was to be sympathetic whenever people would say anything nasty:

'Instead of fighting them, I would say: '*You seem so upset, and I know that's not what you wanted to have happen tonight. Let's talk about your problem*'.'

Setting up

Prepare some examples of members of a live audience purposefully interrupting stand-up comedians with witty or aggressive comments ('heckles') – or collect your own – and write these on cards.

Some suggested examples are given opposite.

Step by step

- Tell your class about the 'esprit d'escalier' predicament:
  - ☐ Has this happened to them?
  - ☐ When?

- Tell the learners that one way to deal with unpleasant remarks is to disregard, or flout, your expected understanding of these remarks – by expressing your sympathy for the speaker.

- Divide the class into pairs or small groups and give each a sample of heckles directed at stand-up comedians.

- Ask the groups to come up with sympathetic comebacks.

- Once everyone has finished, ask the groups to share these with the class and vote on which ones they think are the funniest – or the most effective.

Signing off

Ask your class to compile a list of how not to be rude when speaking to speakers of other languages, or speakers whose language ability is not as strong as theirs:

- *Have the learners any personal stories of when a speaker of another language was rude to them?*
- *Have they witnessed someone being rudely spoken to because of an obvious disadvantage in the use of a language?*
- *How should/could they have responded?*

This coat's got better material than you have.

You're not as funny as you think.

Throw me out right now, please.

That was the worst thing I've ever heard!

Listen to you? I'd sooner listen to the Devil.

Oh yes, I remember when I had my first drink too.

Is there no end to your talent?

Come on, how about trying a bit?

Set my people free!

Daley Starr

Emphasising and exaggerating interest

Strategy
Exaggerating importance, to capture the attention of others.

Setting the context
Daley Starr is another character from the British comic magazine *Viz* (see also *Roger Irrelevant* on page 58):
- As an aspiring journalist, he turns the everyday events of his family and friends into sensational scoops.
- His name is a 'play on words' on the sensationalist tabloid *The Daily Star*.

Encouraging your learners to 'sensationalise' everyday events can help them understand how to make stories more appealing to others.

When writing articles in language assessment tests, candidates are expected to show an attempt to make the reader want to keep reading:

- The Cambridge Assessment English C2 Proficiency Handbook for Teachers, for example, advises that:
  'a successful article interests and engages the reader, often with some description, narration and anecdote. In some cases, a personal angle will be appropriate, and a catchy title will attract the reader's attention.'
- Cambridge typically require that candidates write articles that are:
  - 140–190 words (B2);
  - 220–260 (C1);
  - 280–320 words (C2).

Setting up
None is necessary.

Step by step
- Ask your learners about the social media platforms they use:
  - *What structure do posts take?*
    - *Twitter*, for example, restricts posts to 280 characters.
  - *How do these posts grab the learners' attention?*
  - *What do the learners and 'friends' usually write about on social media?*
- Tell the learners how – in the same way as social media posts – writers of sensationalist newspaper stories try to capture the readers' attention with:
  - a catchy headline;
  - an enticing introductory paragraph, or 'hook';
  - the use of the kind of language (eg colloquialisms and informal structures) that will help them connect with the reader.
- Ask the class to look at the posts made by their 'friends' on social media and to select a couple of stories to work with:
  - These can be as mundane as enjoying a meal at a restaurant, or a dog's birthday.
- As an individual writing task, ask the learners to write some catchy headlines and enticing first lines for these stories.
- When everyone has finished, ask them to read these to the class:
  - *What strategies did the learners use to draw attention to their stories?*

Signing off
As a controlled writing task, ask your learners to choose one of their stories and continue the article, emphasising and exaggerating.

Puntastic punters

Using context and meaning to connect with others

Strategy
Encouraging creative wordplay while considering how words are used in context.

Setting the context
Once, at a teaching conference, I had a lively conversation with teacher trainer Jen Taylor's husband Neil, a man recognised for his love of puns – a playful use of words that exploits their different meanings in context.

- We were waiting for Jen to come out of a workshop, and we discussed having lunch at a seafood restaurant. The conversation ran something like this:
  - 'We should dolphinately take the oppor-tuna-ty.'
    'For cod's hake, yes.'
    'Fin-tastic!'
    'OK, let's mullet over.'

- We were in fits of laughter while those around us cringed:
  - 'What's wrong?' Neil asked them. 'You teachers are supposed to enjoy such word plaice!'

Including puns in conversation *may* endear the hearer to a speaker and subsequently be an entertaining in-group game – qualifying it as a 'positive politeness' strategy:

- But an *overuse* of puns between two speakers could also have the *opposite* effect – resulting in excluding others and bordering on the annoying.

Setting up
None is necessary.

Step by step
- Tell the class some of the jokes opposite:
  - ☐ *Why are they funny – or not?*

- Ask the class to find examples in the jokes of:
  - homophones (words that *sound* the same but have different meanings and spellings – eg *buoys* and *boys*, *B* and *bee*);
  - homographs (words that are *written* the same but have different meanings – eg *ground*, *field*).

- Tell the learners that the example jokes are *puns* that:
  - depend on the different possible meanings of a word;
  - sound alike but have different meanings.
  - ☐ Used in moderation, they can make the speaker seem clever and funny.

- Why do dogs float in water?
  Because they're good buoys.

- Why is it hard to explain things to kleptomaniacs?
  Because they always take things literally.

- What do you call a cow with no legs?
  Ground beef.

- What do you call an alligator in a vest?
  An investigator.

- What do you call a bee that comes from America?
  A USB.

- Why did the scarecrow win an award?
  Because he was outstanding in his field.

- To help the class come up with more, ask them to search online for examples of homophones and homographs.

- When your learners have a few examples:
  - ☐ *Can they think of contexts where both words could be used? (eg a bored board of directors; a wave of enthusiasm at sea …)*
  - ☐ *Can they put them together – either in a joke or short story?*

- When everyone has finished, ask for volunteers to share their jokes or stories with the class.

Signing off
Ask your learners to either look at word lists they have written in the past or to compile semantic fields for particular subjects.

As they do so, they should think about how these words, or related idioms, might be used in *other* contexts:

- A list of animals, for example, may include: *hound*, *horse* (around), *wolf* (down), (lost) *sheep*.
- Foods may include: (big) *cheese*, *butter* (someone up), (a smart) *cookie*, *a piece of cake*.
- Weather conditions may include: *rain* (check), *snowed* (under), *cloud* (nine), *a breeze*.

Ask them:
- *Can they turn any of these into jokes – by putting the meaning from one context into another?*

It takes one to know one

Building class rapport by sharing impressions

Strategy

Guessing the characteristics and interests of others, based on what we think we perceive – in the context of the classroom.

Setting the context

Identifying and explaining the behaviour and preferences of others seems to be one of our major occupations.

We all attempt to 'explain' our differences:
- cultural identity;
- political or religious opinions;
- the arrangement of the stars when someone was born
- which learning style they seem to favour (multiple intelligences, VAK);
- whether someone uses more of the left or right hemispheres of their brains …

But this can lead to division and prejudice.

Care needs to be taken when sharing such impressions:
- The intention of this activity is to build classroom rapport by getting the learners to share their impressions of their classmates.
- You may, however, prefer to work with photographs of people from the news or who have a claim to fame but are unknown to the class.

Setting up

None is necessary.

Step by step

- Ask your learners to write down the names of each person in the class on a piece of paper.
- For large classes, divide the class into two or three groups, and get each group to write down the names of the others in the same group.
- Write three of the following on the board:

  food   car   hobby   music   animal   film   holiday

- Ask the class or group to make notes individually:
  - *What do they believe is the favourite food, car, etc, of each person on their list?*

- When everybody is ready, ask one learner in the class or group to volunteer to be first:
  - *The volunteer should remain silent and listen as the others discuss the notes they made about him or her.*

- When everyone has said what they believe to be true of that learner, ask the learner:
  - *Who was closest?*
  - *What was right?*
  - *What was wrong?*

  Usually, what happens is that the learner will tell the class more about him/herself than the exercise actually requires.

- Repeat the above stages with other volunteers.

Signing off

Ask the class to discuss how marketers use music, images, activities – and maybe even humour – to appeal to a generational or social niche.

The learners should consider how products such as foods (eg breakfast cereals, sweets, etc), cars, toys, etc are promoted to a target audience:
- *Do they think advertisers are successful in the generalisations they make?*
- *Can they think of good or bad examples – perhaps giving personal stories of how they have been influenced by an advert pitched directly at their age to buy something?*
- *Does the language used in such adverts also differ, according to who the advertisers are trying to appeal to – depending on the age, sex or interests of the potential buyer?*

Comic strip(tease)

Matching comic discourse to context

Strategy
Recognising how language is understood differently according to context – where and how misunderstandings can happen – and their comical implications.

Setting the context
Comic strips often depend on the reader's ability to see the humour of how language is used and understood by different speakers in different contexts:
- In Charles M. Schulz' cartoon *Peanuts*, for example, the amusement of Charlie Brown's brilliantly simple catchphrase 'Good grief' depends on the reader's ability to understand him.

In this activity, the learners are given decontextualised statements from cartoons:
- They consider their meaning.
- They put them back into the context they came from, using the original pictures.

Setting up
Collect a selection of comic strips or use the examples opposite (there is also a third cartoon on the website).

Ideally, each one should show characters in different situations (some popular examples could be Peanuts, Garfield, Asterix, etc):
- Number each strip, for later reference.
- Remove the words, for example by scanning and using a graphics editor such as *Microsoft Paint*, and compile these in a separate list – to give to each learner as a Worksheet.

Step by step
- Give the list of phrases to the learners – without saying where these came from.
- Ask the learners to read each phrase and discuss the context:
  - *Who was the speaker?*
  - *Who were they speaking to?*
  - *How were they feeling at the time of speaking?*
- Give the learners the Worksheet, and tell them that the phrases were all taken from these comic strips:
  - *Can they put them back into the pictures?*

There may be more than one possibility.

- Discuss the learners' choices together:
  - *Can they explain the reasons for their choices?*
  - *Why do they think the comic is funny?*
- Now give the learners a copy of the original comic, for them to compare this to the answers they discussed:
  - *Did they find any words confusing or ambiguous?*

Signing off
Ask the learners to find examples of, and share, cartoons or memes that poke fun at the use of language or cultural context.

A large collection of these can be found with a simple search in *Google Images*. For example:
- **homophones** – words that sound the same but which differ in meaning;
- **puns** – wordplay that depends on the different meanings of words that sound the same;
- **double-entendres** – similar to puns, but with a second, socially awkward, meaning;
- **spoonerisms** – speech errors, often intentional, where corresponding letters or units are exchanged (eg *Is it kisstomary to cuss the bride?*).

In a bar

I'll have a whisky and .... cola! | Why the big pause? | I was born with them.

At the cinema

I'm sorry, but are you a bear? | Yes. What are you doing in the cinema? | Well, I liked the book.

CHAPTER FOUR • BEING LIKED

Hitting the headlines

Recognising ambiguity in newspaper headlines

Strategy
Deducing meaning from key words and phrases.

Setting the context
When composing headlines for a blog post, bloggers have to carefully select a restricted number of key words that will optimise search engine results, while satisfying what is known as the TACT test:

Taste – Attractiveness – Clarity – Truth

This often leads to ambiguity, and the subsequent alternative understandings of the story can lead to much amusement:
- This has popularly been demonstrated in the British panel show *Have I Got News for You!*

Setting up
Search the Internet for some favourite examples of ambiguous headlines, and write each one on a separate card.

You can find these by googling 'ambiguous headlines', or you can use the samples below from the University of Pennsylvania Department of Linguistics.

- Astronaut takes blame for gas in spacecraft
- Squad helps dog bite victim
- Drunk gets nine months in violin case
- Drunk drivers paid $1,000 in fall
- Include your children when baking cookies
- Kids make nutritious snacks
- Man struck by lightning faces battery charge
- March planned for next August
- Queen Mary having bottom scraped
- Rugby team's coach set on fire
- Stadium air conditioning fails – fans protest
- Enraged cow injures farmer with axe
- Milk drinkers are turning to powder

Step by step
- Write the following on the board:

  Stolen painting found by tree

- Tell the class that it is an ambiguous headline, and ask the learners why it is ambiguous:
  - In this case, it is not clear whether the 'by tree' modifier refers to where the painting was found, or who found the painting.
  - This is known as a 'dangling modifier'.
- Divide the class into groups of three or four.
- Tell them that they are going to play a game.
- Tell the groups that that you will give each group a card with an ambiguous headline:
  - *Can they discuss how many stories they can make from the headline?*
- They take it in turns to present their stories to the class.
- You award the groups one point for each alternative story.
- At the end of the game, go over the headlines once more:
  - *Can the learners suggest ways to make the headlines more attractive and clear?*

Signing off
Ask the class to search online for advice about how to write headlines:
- *What criteria – besides TACT – can they find?*

If they have websites or blogs:
- *Do their own headlines meet these criteria?*

Chapter Five

Being respected

Please please me

We have looked at *positive politeness* – so, logically, there must also be a '**negative politeness**' strategy.

But don't let these terms mislead you – positive and negative, at least as far as linguistic politeness is concerned, are not opposites, nor does it mean that, because one is negative, it is unfavourable to the other or, in some way, bad.

A good way to understand 'negative', at least in mathematics, as teacher (and one of my uncles) Sverre Wallin once explained to me, would be to think of *heat*:
- A thermometer has both negative and positive temperatures, but unless you are in some way biased to a love of snow or going to the beach, neither can be considered worse than the other.

The same is true of language.

While positive politeness might be considered a socially 'warm' approach, negative politeness might be considered 'cold' and impersonal – instead of concerning itself with establishing rapport with the hearer, it acts as a form of self-protection from any possible imposition upon the hearer.

A request which starts with the words *'I hate to be a nuisance'*, for example, supposedly clears the path for the speaker to cause inconvenience and annoyance – they have already warned us that they would!

The activities in this chapter look at diplomacy, and putting things in such a way that the speakers get what they want – unimpeded.

Sorry seems to be the hardest word

Using 'sorry' as a hedging device in different contexts

Strategy
Using *sorry* to 'soften' utterances.

Setting the context
A viral meme says:
- *'You're not a true Canadian until you have apologised for saying sorry too much!'*

While this may not be true, it does make the point that, in some English-speaking cultures, the word 'sorry' can be used often excessively to minimise the imposition when:
- interrupting:
  - *Sorry, can I just jump in?*
- invading another's space:
  - *Sorry, can I squeeze past?*
- expressing empathy:
  - *I'm so sorry for your loss.*
- making excuses:
  - *Sorry I'm late.*
- drawing attention to something:
  - *Sorry, but are you aware …?*
- fostering trust:
  - *Sorry I doubted you.*

There are many more situations – sometimes even to the annoyance of the hearer!

Setting up
Choose a listening script from any coursebook, and make a copy for each learner.

Step by step
- Ask the learners to tell you as many contexts they can think of when they would use the word *sorry* in English.
- Give each learner a copy of your listening script to read through on their own.
- Ask them to enter the word *sorry* in as many places as they think it could occur.
- The learners read the script together and share their ideas:
  - Where do they think 'sorry' sounds natural?
  - Where does it sound inappropriate?
  - Why?
  - What functions does it perform?
  - Is it an apology or excuse?
  - Is it an adjective – or something else?
- Ask the learners:
  - Which uses of 'sorry' do they think they might adopt in future?
  - Which not?
  - Where do they think it is natural and friendly?
  - Where is it just annoying or silly?

Signing off
Ask the learners to search *YouTube* for 'sorry', and see what results they come up with.

If they find song lyrics or comedy sketches:
- *How is the word used?*
- *What words does it typically collocate with?*
  For example:
  - so sorry;
  - very sorry;
  - say sorry …

A guided tour of the news

Using tact and sensitivity to maintain the hearer's interest

Strategy
Explaining sensitive subjects neutrally, to compensate for a lack of subject knowledge.

Setting the context
Describing situations can be complicated, especially when those situations are also of a sensitive nature. For this reason, teachers and publishers have been warned to avoid subjects such as politics, alcohol, religion, sex, narcotics, isms (*communism*, for example) and pork – collectively known as PARSNIP (see also *Here is the news* on page 70).

But while it may often be easiest to *avoid* a topic and hope it goes away, it is often impossible to do so:
- as such an avoidance of the topic could give the false impression that the speaker is either not aware of a situation, or purposefully being dishonest by trying to hide something.
- and when this is the case, the speaker is faced with the challenge of maintaining the respect of the hearer and explaining events in a way that is neutral and informative.

By avoiding the topics we find difficult to discuss, are we not – as teachers/instructors/guides – doing our learners a disservice?

Setting up
Collect a sufficient number of English language newspapers, so that there is one each for each pair of learners:
- These work especially well if the pairs speak different languages and only one of the learners understands what is written.

If newspapers are not available, a news website with plenty of pictures works equally well.

If the learners have the same interests or jobs, you might want to work with more specialised magazines or e-zines.

Step by step
- Ask your class about the week:
  - *Do the learners like to keep up with the news?*
  - *Which recent news stories have they heard and can tell the class about?*
  - *Which countries and people would they expect to read about, if they looked in the day's newspaper?*
- Divide the class into pairs and ask one learner-volunteer to be the 'guide', while the other will be the 'hearer'.
- Tell the *guides* that they will be given a newspaper to show to the hearers.
- As they do so, they should explain what the photos show, and what the accompanying stories are about:
  - If they do not know much about the story, they shouldn't worry – they can try to hide this from the hearer by glimpsing at the accompanying text.
  - If the hearer asks questions that the speaker/guide cannot answer, they should try not to show that they do not know – but attempt to hide this by making something up, or pretending not to have heard and changing the subject.
  - If they feel strongly about a topic, they don't have to share this fact – they can simply explain the story.
- Tell the *hearers* that they can ask questions – but not directly challenge any of the guides' opinions or beliefs.
- They should make notes (keeping them hidden) about the language the guides use, particularly if the words and expressions help them to answer the questions below:
  - *Which news story is the guide not interested in?*
  - *Which topics in the newspaper does the guide not know much about?*
  - *Which stories is the guide particularly careful or diplomatic with?*
  - *When is the guide making things up?*
- When the guides finish, ask the hearers to share their notes with them.
- Then ask the pairs to exchange roles and re-circulate the newspapers.
- Now give the pairs a newspaper to look through together:
  - *Which topics did they share a common interest in – and which not?*

This can be a useful reference for choosing materials and topics for future lessons.

Signing off
Ask your learners to watch or listen to an episode of the news in English:
- *How do the newscasters report events in a neutral way?*
- *How do their reporting styles differ from those that your learners used?*
- *How does the tone vary, according to the content of the story?*

Plain sailing

Using politically correct language

Strategy
Using politically correct language to express needs and expectations.

Setting the context
Writing job advertisements for newspapers or online recruitment sites calls for politically correct language:
- Employers need to consider the right candidate for their teams but, at the same time, need to think carefully about the language they use to publicly announce this.

Perhaps this is nowhere more crucial than when searching for someone to work with – in a tiny confined space, and possibly for weeks at a time:
- In a marina in Gibraltar, a newsagent used to display job ads for keen sailors to join a tiny crew: perhaps to sail a private yacht into the Mediterranean or out across the Atlantic.

Setting up
None is necessary.

Step by step
- Divide the class into small groups or pairs.
- Explain that they are going to sail across the Atlantic in a zero-emissions yacht – one that relies on the environment (solar panels, underwater turbines, etc) for its power. This will mean being confined together for about a week, perhaps in a life-threatening situation:
  - *To what extent do they think such a trip would take them out of their comfort zones?*
  - *What problems would they envisage?*
- Now explain that they are one person short – and they need to advertise to recruit an additional crew member:
  - *What requirements do they have?*
- They should consider the following points:
  - *What bad/annoying habits do they want to avoid?* (Sleepwalking, fear of seagulls …)
  - *What beliefs/opinions will not be constructive to the voyage or will affect crew trust/friendship?* (Obstinacy, dogmas, belief in conspiracy theories …)
  - *Dietary requirements?* (Must be able to eat fish.)
  - *What skills are necessary?* (Must be able to swim.)
- Ask the learners:
  - *How can they express their needs in a politically correct job announcement?*
- Now ask them to write their announcements.
- When they have finished, ask the groups to put these up around the room. The learners then walk around the room and read each announcement:
  - *Which appeals to them the most?*
  - *Why?*
  - *Are there any points mentioned that they take offence at?*

Signing off
Once the learners have chosen their announcements, you may want to hold class interviews where the groups interview potential candidates.

They can then take a recruiting decision.

CHAPTER FIVE • BEING RESPECTED

The name of the game

Effects of the noun phrase

Strategy
Understanding the power of nominalisation.

Setting the context
Nominalisation, the process of turning verb phrases into noun phrases, is a typical feature of formal English – such as academic writing and legal language.

It distances the speaker from the hearer, and expresses neutrality – which makes it a useful 'negative politeness' strategy.

Setting up
Cut out the cards at the end of this activity – or prepare cards with words of your own – so that you have one for each learner.

Each card contains a verb that can also be converted into a noun, using typical endings – such as:

-ion   -ment   -al   -age   -ing   -ance   -dom

Step by step
- Write the following sentences on the board:
  Speaker A: *The teacher will have no tolerance for the use of mobile phones in the classroom.*
  Speaker B: *I will have no tolerance for your use of mobile phones in the classroom.*
  Speaker C: *I will not tolerate you using your mobile phone in the classroom.*
- Ask the learners what differences they notice, besides first and third person, between the sentences:
  - *Are all the sentences clear?*
  - *Is the first sentence an instruction for the class, for the teacher or for both?*
  - *Which sentence or sentences are the learners most likely to pay attention to? Why?*
  - *Which speaker (A, B or C) do they think is the angriest?*
- Explain to the class:
  - Speaker A uses nouns, which is therefore more typical of formal written English – such as legal language and business correspondence.
  - Speaker B still uses the noun phrase, but addresses the individual as 'you'. There is no doubt about who the hearer is, but the speaker still wishes to maintain a distance from the hearer(s).
  - Speaker C uses verbs – and is therefore more informal.
- Ask the class:
  - *Is this also a characteristic of their first language?*
- Now tell the learners that you will give everyone a card with a verb:
  - They should try to remember the noun that corresponds to their verb, and write a formal rule, perhaps for a code of conduct, for the class.
  - They should write their sentence on the reverse of the card.
- Pin these on the wall.
- Ask the learners to read the statements and to discuss – to see if they agree.

Signing off
In an article for the the *New York Times* Opinionator Blog, author Henry Hitchings gives the following as 'annoying' examples of nominalisation:
- *'Do you have a solve for this problem?'*
- *'Let's all focus on the build.'*
- *'That's the take-away from today's seminar.'*

In each of the above examples, the noun form (eg *solve*, instead of 'solution'; *build* instead of 'building') has not changed from the verb.

Tell the learners that these usages are new or colloquial and may not stand the test of time:
- *Can they think of similar examples in other languages that they speak?*

Reference
Hitchings, H 'Those-irritating-verbs-as-nouns'
https://opinionator.blogs.nytimes.com 30/03/2013

satisfy	enjoy	commit
approve	waste	live
ignore	free	express
disagree	respect	consider

The Spaghetti Challenge

The language of collaboration and leadership

Strategy
Suggesting and instructing teams, employing diplomacy and tact.

Setting the context
In his TED talk at *ted.com*, Peter Skillman shares his observations of different groups of people participating in the 'Spaghetti Challenge':
- This is a contest to see who can build the tallest free-standing structure using only spaghetti sticks, Sellotape® and string, with a marshmallow on the top.

The task is a valuable team-building exercise: it forces people to collaborate – fast!

The most adept, Skillman says, are groups of primary-aged children:
- They do not waste time seeking power (nor use the 'politeness strategies' that this involves – see page 25).
- They do not sit around talking about the problem.

For our own purposes as teachers, the Spaghetti Challenge can be a very useful 'tool' to observe the language that our learners use when working in teams – depending on their relationship to one another.

Setting up
Collect 20 sticks of spaghetti, one metre of string, one metre of Sellotape® and a marshmallow – for each group of four learners.

Step by step
- Tell your class that you would like them to work in groups to complete a challenge – to see who can build the tallest free-standing structure:
  - Skillman suggests that teams be given 18 minutes.
- Divide the class into groups of four, and give them the materials.
- As the groups work to complete their structures, listen carefully to the language that they use, and take notes:
  - *Does any group member take the lead?*
  - *If so, how do they do this?*
  - *What structures do the learners use to make suggestions?*
  - *Do they use positive or negative politeness structures?*
- Once the challenge is over and the winning group has been congratulated, show your class the notes you made, by writing up the sentences they used to make suggestions:
  - *Would they feel comfortable using these with different people – where perhaps the power distance varies:*
    – *their teacher/boss?*
    – *a stranger on the street?*
    – *a brother/sister?*

Signing off
Watch Peter Skillman's talk or Tom Wujec's follow-up – both on *ted.com* – about the Spaghetti Challenge:
- *How does what Peter Skillman says about kindergarteners, or Tom Wujec says about his teams, compare to your learners' experiences of doing the task?*
- *What other things do the videos tell the learners about collaboration?*

References
Skillman, P *Peter Skillman Marshmallow Design Challenge* (Original Design Challenge: 2006) 2014
https://www.youtube.com/watch?v=1p5sBzMtB3Q
Wujec, T *Build a tower, build a team* TED 2010
https://www.ted.com/talks/tom_wujec_build_a_tower_build_a_team?language=en

CHAPTER FIVE • BEING RESPECTED

You are (not) cordially invited …

Recognising ostensible speech acts

Strategy
Understanding why we want to appear to be genuine – even when we are not.

Setting the context
A colleague who was brought up as a bilingual English/German speaker in Germany eventually went to Britain, and was immediately amazed by how friendly everyone was:
- It was only later that she realised many of the invitations that had been made – and the questions about her wellbeing – were not as sincere as they had appeared to be.

'Ostensible' speech acts are a kind of linguistic wolf in sheep's clothing:
- Disguising themselves as invitations, compliments, offers, questions, apologies and assertions, they achieve their purpose by deceiving the poor hearer.

For example, 'We must have lunch sometime' does not always mean we must have lunch!

Setting up
Cut out one set of the cards opposite for each pair of learners.

Step by step
- Write the following statements on the board:
  - With this ring, I thee wed.
  - I arrest you in the name of the law.
  - 5, 4, 3, 2, 1, 0 … all engines running, lift-off, we have a lift off! (from a recording of the Apollo 11 launch)
  - Going once, going twice, sold.

- Ask the class:
  - *Do they recognise these phrases and the speakers?*

- Tell the learners that, in saying each of these phrases, the speaker is also performing a function – ie getting married, arresting, launching a rocket, and selling:
  - This is why phrases like these are called 'speech acts'.

- Now add to the list on the board: 'Have a nice day.'

- Tell the class that many people do not like this phrase:
  - In the UK it may be considered false, an American cliché, or both – if said by a cold-calling salesperson who doesn't really care what day you have!
  - Despite its insincerity, this phrase can also be a *speech act*, used to end a conversation and say goodbye.
  - For this reason, it is known as an 'ostensible' speech act.

I apologise for being late!	How are you?	You look great!
Congratulations on winning.	Shall I give you a lift home?	I'll see what I can do.
I'm sorry you feel that way.	You must meet my dad.	We'll be in touch.

- Tell the class that there are a number of similar phrases (eg an invitation, question or compliment):
  - The speakers assume that the hearers will understand that the phrases are insincere and follow:
    - a 'sequence of pretense' by the speaker;
    - mutual recognition and an appropriate response (denial, dismissal) by the hearer.
  - Any *further* questions (eg *Really?* or giving a full answer) will lead to ambivalence or even discomfort.
  - While seeming to be superficial and insincere, these phrases have a purpose – beyond simply allowing their speakers to appear 'nice'.

- Give pairs of learners a set of cards each, and tell them to look at each statement and discuss:
  - *How and when can it be insincere?*
  - *In which situations would they hear the statements?*
  - *Why does the speaker say it – ie what is its function?*
  - *What would be an appropriate response?*

- Ask the class:
  - *Do 'hedging' devices (I believe, I doubt, I suggest; possibly, perhaps; modal verbs, etc) make the statement appear more, or less, sincere?*
  - *Can the learners think of more statements – perhaps some they have heard before and were confused by?*

Signing off
Ask the class to search the media for public figures apologising, offering or making assertions officially:
- *Do they think these statements appear to be true – but are not necessarily so?*
- *Why?*
- *What is the speaker of these statements trying to achieve?*

Any kind of *ism*

Cynicism, scepticism, criticism …

Strategy
Recognising a speaker's belief or opinion, by looking for clues of modified vagueness (eg by making cautious claims).

Setting the context
Maintaining the confidence of others, and convincing them of our beliefs, can be a delicate balancing act:
- Whether it's an idea, a product or our personal solution to a problem, we need to show the hearer that what we believe is right.
- At the same time, to gain their confidence, we try to connect with, and be liked by, the hearer.

We show respect for their opinion, by using diplomacy and, hopefully, tact. This is where 'fuzzy language' comes to the rescue, protecting our utterances:
- Hedging devices such as:
  - modal verbs (*should, would,* etc)
  - adverbs (*sometimes, possibly*)
  - 'that' clauses (*it could be the case that* …)

One way to understand how, and when, we use these devices is by looking at the language of *isms*.

Setting up
Select an example of an urban myth or conspiracy theory, perhaps by searching online. Famous examples are the idea:
- that the Earth is flat;
- that the moon landing was a hoax.

Step by step
- Write 'ism' on the board, and ask the learners to tell you any words that they can think of that use these letters as a suffix. For example:
  - Hinduism
  - professionalism
  - racism
  - communism
  - Darwinism
  - pragmatism
  - metabolism
- Write up their examples, leaving a space for further words at the top.
- Check that all the learners are familiar with the expressions, and ask:
  - *Do any of the words not belong on the list?*
- Remove any words that are not a practice, belief, ideology or movement:
  - Some words may have alternate meanings in very specialised areas:
    - *pragmatism* being a philosophical movement while *pragmatics* is a linguistic subfield;
    - *metabolism* being a series of chemical reactions as well as an architectural style inspired by this process.
  - Unless your learners have an in-depth knowledge of the different references, focus on the ones that are generally *understood*.
- Add the following three words at the top of the board:
  - cynicism
  - scepticism
  - criticism
- Check that the class know the differences between these last words on the board:
  - A *sceptic*, for example, can be convinced – if presented with sufficient evidence.
  - A *cynic* is more closed-minded, and will not be convinced – regardless of evidence.
- Ask the learners which *isms* involve a prejudice or hatred of others, eg racism, sexism …
  - Also remove these.
- Now present your urban myth or conspiracy theory.
- Give the learners a brief background to the 'story', and write on the board three sentences that reflect the cynic, the sceptic and the critic:
  - *Nonsense. It's not true!*
  (cynic)
  - *I rather doubt it. The facts seem quite unreliable.*
  (sceptic)
  - *That's a sweeping statement, it depends what you mean.*
  (critic)
- Ask the learners to try writing sentences about the story – to reflect the other *isms* on the board:
  - *What would a communist say?*
  - *What would a Darwinist say?*

Any kind of *ism*

- Once they have finished, point out the language differences between the sceptic (eg *rather*, *seems*, *quite*) and the cynic, who is very direct:
  - ☐ Remind the class that scepticism is regarded as more open-minded and positive than cynicism.

- Reflect together on the language used by the speakers of each of the sentences that your learners wrote:
  - ☐ *Do your learners think their statements are direct or vague?*
  - ☐ *Does the speaker use any words that express hesitation or non-commitment (hedging devices)?*
  - ☐ *How sure is the speaker of each sentence?*
  - ☐ *How can the learners tell?*

Signing off

Ask your learners to further consider the language used by conspiracy theorists – by searching online for articles that support the theory that you looked at in class:

- *How certain are the writers of what they say?*
- *How does the language they use reflect this?*
- *Do the learners think that the writers provide sufficient plausible evidence to back up what they say?*
- *Are the learners convinced? Why/why not?*

Mincing your words

Minimising objectionable words or profanity

Strategy
Understanding how recreating sounds is used to create 'minced oaths' – acceptable alternatives to profane or blasphemous terms – and avoid offending the hearer.

Setting the context
People who use more profanity are more trustworthy than those who don't!

At least, that's what four researchers set out to prove in a combined study by the universities of Maastricht, Hong Kong, Stanford and Cambridge.

While the language of profanity does cause offence, it does not necessarily follow that it is intended to aggravate or attack the hearer:

- On the contrary, in many contexts, such language is intended to 'express one's genuine feelings' and is associated with 'higher integrity at the society level' – where it often also helps the speaker to connect, build rapport (see 'positive politeness' on page 25) and establish sympathy with the hearer.
- To understand how it does so, we need look no further than how the creators of popular fictional characters in cinema and literature use minced oaths to engage the audience, and even endear them to their characters – '*Suffering succotash!*' in the words of Sylvester the Cat.

English includes many such examples of perfectly acceptable, and often funny, examples of 'false swearing'.

All that is needed for this is some basic wordplay – rhyming and alliteration, for example, which use the same groups of letters or sounds as the more objectionable terms:

- *Gosh!*
  (God)
- *Crikey!*
  (Christ kill me)
- *Jeepers Creepers!*
  (Jesus Christ)
- *Darn and tarnation!*
  (damnation)
- *Heck!*
  (hell)
- *Sugar!*
  (sh*t)

You will see our own reluctance to write one of the words in full – to avoid offending anyone or any embarrassed blushes!

And we can't forget the delightful array of 'f' words: *flip, fork, fudge, fiddlesticks …*

Mincing your words

Setting up
Prepare a list of the example situations given opposite of this activity, or any others that you can think of, so that there is one for each group.

Step by step
- Write the following six statements, and their speakers, in a 'mix and match' exercise on the board:
    - By Toutatis!
    - Great Krypton!
    - Thank the Maker!
    - Merlin's pants!
    - Rats!
    - Well, blow me down!

    Answers:
    - Asterix
    - Superman
    - C-3PO
    - Harry Potter
    - Charlie Brown
    - Popeye

- Check the answers together, and ask the learners:
    - *Can they say what the above lines tell us about their speakers?*
    (origin, beliefs, age, era, etc)
    - *Can they identify, though not necessarily repeat, the offensive utterances that they replace?*
    (blasphemous, sexual or other references, etc)
    - *Can they tell you why the statements are more appropriate for the characters – better than actual profanities?*
    - *Can they say what other, similar, minced oaths they have heard in other languages that they speak or have seen used by other characters – and in what contexts?*
        - 'Shiver me timbers!' (pirates such as Long John Silver)
        - 'Great Scott!' (scientists such as Doc Brown)

- Divide your class into small groups and give them the situations opposite:
    - *Can they write down one or several minced oaths for each one?*
    - *Can they bear in mind common linguistic features, such as rhyming and alliteration?*

- Once everybody has finished, ask the learners to share what they have written with the class.

One of the two pigs – upon seeing the big bad wolf blow down their houses.
Pinocchio – seeing his nose grow after he has just told a lie.
One of the other ducklings – when they discover that their ugly sibling is a swan.
The hare – spotting the tortoise on the finishing line.
Beauty's father – when his daughter brings her beloved Beast home to 'meet the parents'.

Signing off
In his book *The Stuff of Thought*, Steven Pinker says that swearing can be:
- *abusive*
  (insults and intimidation)
- *cathartic*
  (a reaction to pain or negative experience)
- *dysphemistic*
  (using a dysphemism, a derogatory alternative to a more pleasant term, to expresses the speakers' negative impression of something)
- *emphatic*
  (emphasising the scale of something)
- *idiomatic*
  (for no reason other than to create an informal context)

Depending on the class, and your relationship with the learners, you may wish to discuss examples of the above together.

References
Feldman, G, Lian, H, Kosinski, M and Stillwell, D 'Frankly, we do give a damn: The relationship between profanity and honesty' *Social Psychological and Personality Science* 1 (11) 2017

Pinker, S *The Stuff of Thought – Language as a Window into Human Nature* Penguin Books 2007

Sofian's game

Using and understanding euphemisms

Strategy
Rephrasing sensitive words and using metaphor to appear kinder or to be more politically correct.

Setting the context
Using the simplest words may be good for clarity, but often be seen as too direct, or even cruel, for the listener's ears.

When I suggested to my class that we look at this language together, and discuss their alternative euphemisms – words that the Germans refer to as *Beschönigung*, or 'sugarcoating' (for more about euphemisms, see also *A royal bastard* on page 80) – my learner Sofian suggested we turn the whole thing into a game.

Setting up
None is necessary.

Step by step
- Tell your learners that you are going to write an offensive word on the board:
  - Warn them that if they are easily offended they should look away now!
- Write: *Toilet*
- Now ask the class if they are offended.
- Explain that, for some English-speaking cultures (for example, American), this word needs to be avoided.
- Ask the class to suggest any alternatives that they know. They could include:
  - restroom
  - loo
  - WC
  - ladies' room / men's room
- Explain that all of these are attempts to make something sound 'nicer'.
- Now write the following words in a row across the board:

  stupid   fat   old   ugly   boring

- Remind the learners that these can apply to different things, and not just people:
  - a stupid idea
  - a fat bonus
  - an old car
  - an ugly landscape …
- Ask the class to suggest any alternative words or expressions that they know for them.

  These could include:

  not bright   overweight   senior   disappointing   dull

- Write all the expressions that you collect under the word for which it is a synonym:
  - It does not matter how informal or colloquial they are.
- Reflect on the words collected.
- Divide the learners into groups of three or four.
- Tell them that you will give them more expressions, to play a game to see who can guess what they mean.
  - *a sandwich short of a picnic* (stupid)
  - *as dim/bright as a 40-Watt light bulb* (stupid)
  - *husky* (fat)
  - *horizontally challenged* (fat)
  - *vertically challenged* (short)
  - *long in the tooth* (old)
  - *no spring chicken* (old)
  - *the perfect face for a radio star* (ugly)
  - *a wonderful personality* (ugly)
  - *like watching paint dry* (boring)
  - *dull as dishwater* (boring)
- Ask the learners which they found easy, and which were funny:
  - *Can they explain the origin of some of the meanings?*
    - 'no spring chicken' – 18th-century chickens born in the spring fetched a much higher price than those that had gone through the winter;
    - finding yourself in the *husky* section of a clothes shop.
  - *Are some of them very similar in a language that your learners also speak?*

Signing off
Ask the learners to look out for more examples of euphemisms (perhaps in job announcements) or translate into English those they use in their own language.

Chapter Six

Being indirect

I am the walrus

In this chapter, things get awkward!

Rather than worry about whether the things we say will make us unpopular or lose respect, let's avoid saying them at all!

Whether it is a cultural discomfort with regard to saying the word 'no' – or something of a more delicate nature – we can disguise our utterances with euphemism, clever wordplay, innuendo, overtone, undertone, nuance and slurs.

This chapter introduces learners to subtle hints, implied meaning, idioms – and everything else that has the power to confuse and mislead.

By saying things '**off record**' – and relying on the hearer to come up with the correct interpretation – we can be critical *constructively*, aggressive *passively* and assertive *indirectly*.

Should things not go according to plan, we can plead, in our defence, that we never meant whatever it was that we are accused of saying – because we didn't say it!

We can say it is the hearer's fault for having got the wrong end of the (linguistic) stick.

Or, of course, we can be *very* direct – and say nothing at all!

Ambiguous appraisals

Being diplomatic, to mask unfavourable feedback or criticism

Strategy
Using ambiguity when disguising criticism.

Setting the context
Writing job references, or appraising others critically, can be problematic – particularly when a colleague or employee has performed poorly.

While it may be necessary to warn a prospective employer of an employee's unsatisfactory performance, in some countries employers can be sued for any negative statements or character defamation.

One solution to this dilemma is *ambiguity*, and the hope that the reader will be able to interpret and understand what is meant.

Setting up
Search the Internet for 'ambiguous reference letters', or use the examples given in the grid opposite.

Step by step
- Write the words below on the board:

  interesting   unbelievable   amazing

- Ask the learners:
  - *How many contexts can they think of for these words?*
  - *How does intonation change their meaning?*
  - *What problems might be created if there is no intonation – for example, in writing?*

- Ask the learners about job references:
  - *Have they ever had to write one for a bad employee?*
  - *How carefully did they think about the words that they used?*
  - *How did they approach difficult or negative issues?*

- Give the example:
  'All his job appraisal comments could be summed up in one word: *interesting / unbelievable / amazing*.'

- Ask the class:
  - *Why are these words ambiguous?*

- Give the learners examples of ambiguous statements (see opposite), and ask them to list two interpretations: one favourable and one unfavourable.

I, the undersigned, have worked with the applicant for two years, which I know I will never forget.
She left her stamp on our business. Now it is time she stamps on yours.
We strongly recommend you give the applicant what she deserves.
There is a thin line between brilliance and madness, and I can testify that this man is firmly on one side of that line.
We can honestly say that this member of staff is in a league of her own, leaving her colleagues shaking their heads in amazement.
When she announced she was leaving our employment, a wave of emotion swept through our premises.

Signing off
As a homework – or self-reflection – task, ask the learners to either write (or search online for) a review of a product or service they recently used.

Can they re-write any poor feedback – using words or phrases which could be understood differently?

Getting the learners to consider the ambiguity of words can help them to avoid any potential misunderstandings in future correspondence.

Learners can find more examples of ambiguous job references in my book *Basis for Business C1 Teaching Guide* (Cornelsen, 2nd edn 2021).

An elephant in the classroom

Handling awkward situations

Strategy

Speaking about sensitive issues or topics that require trust or understanding from the hearer.

Setting the context

When the notorious 'street artist' Banksy opened his 'Barely Legal' exhibition in Los Angeles in 2006, his show featured a live elephant:

- Painted in the same pattern as the surrounding wallpaper of the room, it was meant to symbolise the common metaphor of an 'elephant in the room'.

The metaphor refers to something that is blatantly obvious but, due to its sensitive nature, nobody wishes to discuss – and we even pretend that it is not there.

Setting the context, such as breaking bad news or broaching a sensitive subject, call for indirectness – at best, hints and suggestions – with an expectation that the speakers or hearers will know what is implied.

Setting up

Prepare sufficient cards which set different contexts – so that there is one for each group or pair of learners that you form.

There are some suggestions below.

Something only your best friend can tell you.
Explaining the facts of life to a young relative.
Proposing marriage to someone you've recently met.
Warning someone of their prejudice towards someone or something.
Telling a parent/partner that you have decided to become a fruitarian (someone who eats only what falls naturally from a plant).
Asking an older relative not to slurp their soup.

Step by step

- Write the words *awkward moments* on the board, and ask the class to think any about difficult conversations they have had recently:
  - ☐ These could be:
    – breaking some news to a family member or friend;
    – asking someone for help with something.

- Divide the class into pairs or small groups, and tell everyone that you would like them to improvise roleplaying some 'contexts':
  - ☐ They do not have time to prepare their conversations, and should start as soon as they receive a card.
  - ☐ They can hold these conversations simultaneously, or individually in front of the class.

- Let the activity run, looking out for any politeness strategies (see page 25 in Part A) and listening for the language the learners used:
  – A dependence on the hearer's feelings or benefit from a situation (eg creating a feeling of injustice or desire to do something).
  – Modality and conditionals (eg *it could/might be the case …*; *if it were …*).
  – (In)directness (eg using metaphors: *'the birds and the bees', 'gone to meet their maker'*; idioms, etc).
  – Avoiding responsibility or distancing the speaker from the subject (eg use of the passive voice).

- Once the conversations have finished, draw the learners' attention to the language they used, and discuss alternative ways to approach awkward topics.

Signing off

Ask your learners to watch/listen out for how interviewers approach difficult topics in talk shows or political debates:

- The BBC World Service, for example, has a regular TV and radio series (available as regular downloadable podcasts) called *HARDtalk*, where celebrities who are in some way connected to the stories hitting the headlines are asked very direct questions – often off record – about the work that they do.

Ask the learners what they notice about the interviewers' techniques, and discuss these in a future lesson.

Reasons to steer clear

Using sarcasm to (over)emphasise a point

Strategy
Being intentionally contradictory, to remove doubt or misgivings from the hearer's mind.

Setting the context
In an attempt to encourage tourists to visit places off the beaten track, bloggers – and even the tourist boards of such places – have recently started a new line of counterattack against anyone doubting the point of visiting:
- With headlines such as 'reasons NEVER to go to …', they aim to eliminate any doubts you might have.

One such example is:

37 Reasons to Steer Clear of Dumfries and Galloway

It aims to promote a little-known and often-overlooked corner of Scotland, which is arguably equal in beauty to the hugely popular Highlands and Islands.

To entice visitors, it uses phrases such as:
– *Don't even consider Dumfries and Galloway.*
– *It's nothing special, really: just look at …*
– *There are probably too many …*
– *There's nothing for you here.*

These phrases are then accompanied by visually stunning pictures of:
– natural beauty
  (Galloway Forest Park, Mull of Galloway …);
– historic buildings
  (Sweetheart Abbey, Cardoness Castle …);
  etc.

Setting up
Enter the following words in a *Google* search box: 'reasons not to visit'.

Select one of the suggestions that it offers, and save the link or print the page – so that there is a copy for each learner.

Step by step
- To prepare the learners for the language they will need to use, ask your class about the places they have visited but did not enjoy:
  - *What was wrong?*
    – *Was the area polluted or dirty?*
    – *Were the people unfriendly?*
    – *Was there a lack of things to see or do?*
    – *Was the food bad?*

- On the board, compile a class list of these complaints.

- Show the class the article you saved:
  - *What message do the learners think it is trying to convey?*
  - *How does the article make the learners feel (eg foolish – for ever thinking otherwise)?*
  - *Do they find it funny or strange?*
  - *Would it work in their own culture?*
    – *Why?*
    – *Why not?*

- Now ask the learners to work individually or in small groups, to list the positive things about the area where they live or come from.

- Once they have a list, ask them to write a 'negative' text about their area that is similar to the article you showed them:
  - Tell them they can use the sentences on the board, or come up with their own.
  - Ask them to find photographs that show the contrary of what their statements say.

- Ask the learners to share their statements in a *PowerPoint* presentation with the rest of the class, and then to give each other feedback.

Signing off
If your learners are especially pleased with their presentations, and can collect their own photographs, ask them to try sending these to a webzine or blog to publish online.

Seeing their work published can give learners a tremendous motivational boost.

Avoidance charades

Recognising indirect requests

Strategy
Recognising what others want – by interpreting their hints or indirect requests, or by their avoidance of the topic altogether.

Setting the context
How you ask someone to do something for you will depend on a number of factors:
- How well you know the other person.
- The age difference between you.
- Your job title.
- The urgency of the situation …

It also varies, depending on your culture:
- Some societies find it difficult to be direct.
- Others are notorious for being too direct.

In his book *Outliers*, Malcolm Gladwell describes the level of our indirectness as 'sugarcoating' the meaning of what is being said. (See *Sofian's game* on page 109.)

Setting up
Cut out the cards opposite so that you have one class set.

You may wish to add to these with further requests.

Step by step
- Write the following on the board:

  Move!

- Ask the class who might say this, and when:
  - Would they feel comfortable saying it to …
    - the person sitting next to them on the bus?
    - their boss?
    - their teacher?
    - their cat/dog?
    - another road user in traffic?

If the answer is 'no' to any of these:
  - Would the context make a difference …
    - if someone is in their way?
    - if someone is in danger of being hurt by a flying object?

- Tell the class that we can 'mitigate' what we say – on different levels:
  - Instead of 'Move!', for example, we might say …
    - We should move.
    - Could you please move?
    - I don't suppose you could move aside for one moment …
  - And, ultimately, we might hint:
    - It's a bit difficult for me to move …

- Divide the class into two teams.
- Tell them that you will play a game using hints and indirectness to make requests.
- Ask for a volunteer from each team to come and select a card, and explain:
  - They cannot use any of the words on the cards, but can make *hints* to get what they want.
  - The teams should ask questions that lead to an understanding of what the volunteer wants.
- At the end of the game, go through the cards together:
  - How comfortable would the class be asking for these things directly?

Signing off
Ask your learners to search online for what Malcolm Gladwell refers to as 'mitigated speech' – to see how we mitigate the things that we say – and then to compare this to their own correspondence or writing:
- Do they think that they are sometimes guilty of too much 'sugarcoating' – and not being understood, as a consequence?

Reference
Gladwell, M *Outliers: The Story of Success* Little, Brown and Company 2008

You want someone to give you a blanket or lend you their coat.

You want a cup of coffee.

You want to borrow someone's notes to write an essay.

You want someone to help you fix your car.

You want to use your neighbour's phone.

Somebody has taken your seat in the room and you want it back.

You want to ask someone to go to the cinema with you.

Reading between the lines

Effective comprehension and deeper understanding

Strategy

Identifying context and situation from a written or recorded script.

Setting the context

Comprehension questions can often be limiting – in the sense that the learners simply have to find the answer somewhere in the text, without critical thinking.

Instead, by giving the learners only *part* of a conversation – with just a few clues to *who* or *where* the speakers are – and then asking the class to write their own questions, we can help them gain a deeper understanding, as well as giving their motivation a boost.

Setting up

Select a script from a coursebook, video or play of your choice. The language should be appropriate for the level of the learners.

Alternatively, you can use the sample script on page 116.

Step by step

- Divide the class into small groups or pairs.
- Tell them that you will give them a script:
  - *Can they come up with some 'typical' comprehension questions?*
- As they do so, write these on the board.

  From the example text, these could be:
  - *How many degrees does A want B to move?*
    (15 degrees southwards)
  - *What will happen if they do not move?*
    (there will be a collision)
  - *How many destroyers is B escorted by?*
    (six)

  or
  - *Who is A?*
  - *Why is it not possible for A to move?*
  - *What does B mean by 'necessary action'?*

- Explain to the learners:
  - The first three questions above require answers that are given in the script.
  - The second three questions require the readers to use their imaginations and come up with their own answers, using any *clues* provided in the text.

  For these second questions, there is no right or wrong answer:
  - other than they are either *on*, or *airborne over*, the sea.

- Ask the groups to come up with five further questions to add to the first set, and to write these down on a sheet of paper.
- Collect the questions, and redistribute them so that each group is given a new set of questions.
- Ask the groups to answer the questions that they have been given.
- When everybody has finished, ask the learners to share their answers with the class:
  - *Are the answers different?*
  - *What led the groups to make their decisions?*
  - *Was it simply a guess, or did something in the text help them?*
- Finally, tell the class where the script came from, who was speaking, and what the original context was:
  - *Whose answers were closest to the original?*
- If you used the example script on the next page, tell the class that this is from the *YouTube* film 'USS Abraham Lincoln vs lighthouse'*, and show it to the class**:
  - *Did they recognise the story?*
    (It is a very old one, and there are different versions online.)

Signing off

As a self-study task, ask your learners to continue the story that they shared – as a story or as a script.

Help them, by setting questions such as:
- *What happened next?*
- *How did the story end?*

* Real communication between a Galician Maritime Emergency Station in Spain and the U.S. Navy, recorded off the coast of Galicia, October 16 1997, and released for publication by the Spanish Military in March 2005.

** See *https://www.youtube.com/watch?v=KvRYd8U7qGY*

Acknowledgement

Thanks to my friend Harry Kuchah for the inspiration for this activity.

CHAPTER SIX • BEING INDIRECT

Reading between the lines

A: Please change your course by 15 degrees southwards, in order to prevent a collision with us.

B: Change your course by 15 degrees northwards, in order to avert a collision with us.

A: This is not possible. You have to avoid.

B: We are escorted by two cruisers, six destroyers and four submarines. I command you to change your course 15 degrees northwards. If you do not comply, we will be forced to take necessary action.

A: We are two persons. With us we have our dog, we have two beers, we have our food, and a friend who is making a siesta right now. We do not move anywhere.

**Transcript of the video
'USS Abraham Lincoln vs lighthouse'**

Mark my words
Pragmatic discourse markers

Strategy
Using 'discourse markers' to reflect honesty and truthfulness.

The online *Oxford Learner's Dictionary* describes a discourse marker as: 'a word or phrase that organizes spoken language into different parts – for example – *Well* … or … *On the other hand*.'

Discourse markers can also show the speaker's attitude to what he/she is saying – for example: *frankly*, *to be honest*, *but what about …?*

Setting the context
There is a subtle difference between *lying* and *dishonesty* – and the level of how much a speaker is trying to withhold the truthfulness of a story:
- The former aims directly to deceive.
- The latter aims to be 'economical with the truth', and perhaps lessen the shock or outrage towards a story.

Both, however, can be recognised by a number of pragmatic discourse markers that the speaker uses to hide the truth.

Setting up
Consider the interesting things you have learnt about individual learners:
- Are these generally known by the class or things that you have discovered?

If you struggle to think of anything, try to speak to your learners individually in a previous lesson or identify something unique about them – that other class members will not know.

Alternatively, ask them to write something about themselves that they are sure nobody else in the class knows:
- This could be:
  - a visit to another country;
  - the 'baddest' thing they ever did;
  - an amusing confession they would like to make;
  - a famous person they have met …

It is important that you remember who has said what:
- Once you have a collection, write these individual statements on cards.
- The learners will be working in groups:
  - to keep organisation simple, you may wish to decide these groups as you write the cards.

Mark my words

Step by step

- Ask your learners:
  - *How good do they think they are at concealing the truth?*
- Tell them that you will play a game where teams have to guess who is telling the truth and who is making it up.
- Ask the learners to work in groups of four or five.
- To begin the game, give out one card with a statement belonging to one member of that group:
  - Ask the group to read it together.
- Then ask the group to volunteer three of its members:
  - One of them is the 'owner' of that statement (from the individual conversations you had in previous lessons).
  - The other two must use their imaginations to make up a story to try and convince opposing groups that the statement on the card is *their* sentence.
- When ready, ask all three to read the written statement aloud to the class.
- The other groups ask questions:
  - *Can they decide which of the three learners is telling the truth?*
- If the groups correctly identify who is telling the truth:
  - *What gave the other two away?*
  - *Was this because of:*
    - *– a lack of detail?*
    - *– an inconsistency in the story?*
    - *– another reason?*
- The other teams now take turns to read a statement from one of *their* group.
- Ask the learners:
  - *Do they think that the language they used during the game reflects reflects their confidence when they know they are telling the truth?*
  - *Were the 'liars' trying too hard to convince the hearers? Perhaps with give-away phrases such as …*
    - *– 'believe me'*
    - *– 'it's true'*
    - *– 'right'*

Signing off

These discourse markers, or filler words, that we use show consideration of our conversational partners:

- According to Professor Michael Hanford:
  'If you invite somebody to a party and they say no without any of those markers, they will appear rude probably. If you say *'um, well, you know, sorry'* it makes it much more polite. They play a really important politeness function.'

Ask the learners to think about the discourse markers that they know, and perhaps use:

- *Which of these could reflect dishonesty, by trying to convince the hearer that what they say is right?*

Ask them to search online for the discourse markers or 'little words' that give away deception and to share what they discover with the class.

References

Oxford Learner's Dictionary:
https://www.oxfordlearnersdictionaries.com/definition/english/discourse-marker?q=discourse+marker

Hanford, M *The Independent* Online article by Olivia Blair, 'lifestyle reporter':
https://www.independent.co.uk/life-style/um-filler-words-discourse-markers-why-use-er-you-know-a7665721.html

CHAPTER SIX • BEING INDIRECT

Brutally civil
Consciously creating contradictions

Strategy
Understanding oxymorons: lexical chunks, pairs or groups of words that often function as one unit, and that initially appear to contradict each other.

Setting the context
'Why call it a civil war? There's nothing very civil about killing people', my friend Seamie, who enjoys being very silly, teased. (You may remember Seamie from pages 61 and 91.)

He had a point. But the 'civil' here, as he in fact knew, refers not to a synonym for *courteous*:
- It comes from the Latin *civilis* – meaning 'citizen'.

Civil war, like an *open secret*, a *farewell reception* and *bittersweet* are all examples of oxymorons – and they are weirdly normal!

Setting up
None is necessary. However, you might like to prepare a copy of the completed grid on page 119 to refer to.

Step by step
- Write the numbers 1–20 in a grid on the board, as in the example below.

1	2	3	4	5
6	7	8	9	10
11	12	13	14	15
16	17	18	19	20

- Write on the board:

  It is an open secret among the staff.

- Ask your learners what they understand by 'open secret':
  - Do they know it is something that is supposed to be secret, but is known to many people?
- Draw the learners' attention to the fact that *open* and *secret* contradict one another:
  - Words like these are called 'oxymorons': from the Greek *oxus* and *moros* – 'sharply foolish'.

- Tell the learners that they will play a memory game, or pelmanism, to find ten oxymorons.
- Divide the class into small groups of four or five:
  - Point to the grid on the board, and say that each number represents one word.
- The groups each take a turn to call out two numbers and then decide if the combined words make an oxymoron:
  - If a group chooses 2 and 3, remove the numbers and write the corresponding words from the completed grid (*copy* and *myth*).
  – Can this combination make an oxymoron? It can't.
  – So remove the words and replace them once more with just their numbers.
  - If a group chooses 2 and 5 (*copy* and *original*), give them a point for finding 'original copy':
  – Do not replace these words with their numbers – instead, leave them on the board.
  – Offer the group a second point if they can tell you the *context* in which it could be *used*.
  - If a group chooses two words which were not one of the original pairings, but which could still be an oxymoron (eg *definite myth* or *friendly crisis*), only award a point if they convince the class of its meaning.
- The game ends when all of the words on the board have been revealed and used:
  - *Which of the combinations were the class already familiar with?*
  - *Can they be translated into other languages that the learners know?*
  - *Did the learners find any particularly funny?*

Signing off
Ask your class to look out for odd-sounding oxymorons in the media:
– peacekeeping missile,
– humane slaughter,
– only choice …

Or funny/sarcastic examples:
– Microsoft Works
– Jumbo shrimp
– Limitless Ltd …

Share these in future lessons.

Brutally civil

Suggested oxymorons

genuine imitation
friendly takeover
true myth
clearly confused
definite maybe
unbiased opinion
original copy
virtual reality
working holiday
minor crisis

○ Completed grid

1 genuine	2 copy	3 myth	4 reality	5 original
6 maybe	7 unbiased	8 confused	9 imitation	10 clearly
11 holiday	12 working	13 friendly	14 crisis	15 takeover
16 definite	17 virtual	18 opinion	19 minor	20 true

Literally figurative

From graphical representation to meaning

Strategy
Decoding meaning from rebus puzzles, emoticons and abbreviated forms.

Setting the context
How many of us, I wonder, have had to smile …
- as we imagine – on hearing a car navigation system declare 'bear left at the fork' – a big furry animal next to a cutlery tool in the road ahead?
- as we picture – upon hearing the result for a vote in the House of Commons – a bunch of politicians facing one direction while straining to look in another – as the Speaker of the House declares:
'The Ayes (pronounced the same as *eyes*) to the left … The Noes (pronounced the same as *nose*) to the right.'

Such mental images have entertained us since the pharaohs:
- Rebus puzzles, which use a combination of pictures and/or individual letters, numbers and other characters (eg #, *, !) to represent a short phrase, go back to Ancient Egypt – and probably beyond.

In more recent times, they have reappeared in texting, for the sake of convenience.

Setting up
Search the Internet, for example in *Google Images*, for some rebus puzzles:
- Select several that you consider appropriate for your learners' language ability.

Collect these in a handout, and make enough copies so that there is one for each learner.

Alternatively, use the examples given on page 120.

Step by step
- Write the following on the board:
  - *Can the class guess the phrase that it represents?*

  Food   thought   thought   thought   thought

- Explain that it is a puzzle which uses letters and pictures to illustrate a short phrase:
  Food + four 'thought's – 'Food for thought'.

- Give the learners a copy of your handout:
  - *Can they solve the puzzles?*
    You might want to set a time limit for this, and award points for the puzzles solved.

Literally figurative

- Go through the suggested solutions at the end of the activity together with the class:
  - *Which puzzle did they find the easiest/hardest to solve?*
  - *Which characters or 'representations' do they use in their text messages or emails?*

  U   XOXO   L8   ...

  - *Does their use of these depend on context?*
    - social media;
    - business correspondence;
    - age of, or relationship with, the addressee.
  - *Which symbols can the learners use in other languages that they know?*
  - *Which do they think are not translatable?*

Signing off

While words and phrases can be abbreviated or illustrated by characters, the use of such characters may be quite different to what they are *supposed* to represent.

Ask your learners to tell you what LOL means and they will probably tell you someone is 'laughing out loud':
- If you suggest that some might think that it means 'lots of love' – the class will probably tell you this alternative meaning is either rare or out-of-date!

According to linguist John McWhorter, in his TED talk *Txtng is killing language. JK!!!*, LOL means neither: 'It's a marker of empathy. It's a marker of accommodation. We linguists call things like that pragmatic particles.'

Pragmatic particles are words, or expressions, that are used to fill the gaps in discourse – and can have very different uses:
- In texting, LOL may be the equivalent of a 'Pues' at the beginning of a Spanish sentence, or a 'ne' at the end of a German one.
- In English, LOL has the same function as a 'like', 'you know', or the now omnipresent 'literally'.
  'What does literally mean?' Alma
  'Nothing – it's just there.' Andreas

Ask your learners to consider at how and when they use LOL:
- Why do they use it?
- What function does it serve?

Reference
McWhorter, J *Txtng is killing language. JK!!!*, TED 2013
https://www.ted.com/talks/john_mcwhorter_txtng_is_killing_language_jk

Suggested solutions:
under the weather;
land on your/someone's feet;
fall in love;
cut corners;
trip around the world;
meet half way;

serve someone right;
know the ropes;
hang up:
kick the habit:
on the ball;
stir up.

DC Onomatopoeia

Contextualising onomatopoeic words

Strategy
Considering the connection between words and the sounds that they describe.

Setting the context
Onomatopoeia is the name of a DC Comics super-villain and enemy of Batman.

Onomatopoeic words are those which are formed from the sound of whatever it is that they are associated with – examples include:
- *splash* (of a heavy object falling unceremoniously into water);
- *sizzle* (of bacon in the hot oil of a frying pan);
- *woof* (of a dog).

While some words (*bam*, *pow*, *snap*) are obviously sounds, others – such as *cough*, *bark*, *thump* and *flutter* – have become verbs that are frequently used and may not be immediately apparent.

DC's super-villain gets his name from the fact that he only ever says words that imitate the noises around him, such as things breaking, taps dripping, gunshots and crashes.

This activity encourages your learners to use such words – by adding onomatopoeic utterances to everyday conversation – or to descriptive writing, where writers using such expressions are helped to connect with their readers' imaginations.

Setting up
Find and copy a listening transcript from a coursebook or teaching guide.

For this activity, ideally, there should be more than two speakers:
- Transcripts of business meetings work well.
- Or a story which describes a series of events.

Step by step
- Ask your class to suggest sounds they identify with:
  - an explosion (eg *bang*, *boom*, *blast*)
  - a car horn (eg *beep*, *hoot*, *honk*)
  - the dripping or movement of water (eg *drip*, *drop*, *splash*)
  - animals (eg *woof*, *squeak*, *gobble*)
- Ask the class:
  - *Do these differ in the language(s) that your learners speak?*
  - *Do your learners know any alternatives in English?*
    - (tweet, cheep, chirp, peep …)
- Share any sounds that you all know:
  - Animal sounds are often funny.
- Tell the class that many words, like the ones you have already discussed, imitate the sounds of what they describe:
  - This is called *onomatopoeia* :
    - (from the Greek *onoma* for 'name' and *poeia* for 'I make').
- Ask the learners to search online for *onomatopoeic* words, and to write a list of their favourites:
  - They can quiz each other about these words – asking classmates to guess what their words describe.
- Tell the class about the DC Comics character who speaks using only 'onomatopoeic' words.
- Give the learners copies of the transcript or story that you prepared, and ask them to add onomatopoeic words, as if the cartoon character were also in the story:
  - They can do this task individually or in small groups.
- At the end of the task, you may want to read or play the recording of the transcript to the class:
  - As you do so, the learners join in by reading Onomatopoeia's lines aloud.
  - These can be inserted whenever the learners think they are appropriate.

Signing off
Ask your class which of their lines worked well, which were unseemly, and which seemed unnatural:
- *What different effects (eg funny, intrusive, offensive, etc) do the learners think including onomatopoeia has upon the hearer?*
- *Can they identify any examples where the same words are used in different contexts?*
  - The 'murmur', for example, of …
    - *traffic;*
    - *people;*
    - *the earth beneath our feet;*
    - *someone's heart.*

A taboo U-turn

Understanding unexpected collocations

Strategy
Recognising the meaning and context of noun or adjective compounds which, at first sight, may appear contradictory or nonsensical.

Setting the context
Taboo is a very popular word-guessing game, which has also been known to come to the rescue of the unfortunate teacher who may have under-planned for a lesson and runs out of things to do, with some time left until the lesson ends.

The rules are simple, and the game requires little preparation:
- Players are given a word, which they are not allowed to repeat.
- They must then elicit the word from their teammates by describing it.

This activity works a little bit like that, but makes a 'U-turn' from the usual procedure:
- Here, instead of relying on the teams to know the word that is described, they are given an *unfamiliar* word or expression – in the hope that the other players will discover its meaning.

Setting up
Compile a list of unusual collocations that you use regularly.

I have provided some examples of my own opposite.

Step by step
- Write the word *bookworm* on the board and explain that it is a metaphor.
- Ask the class what they think the word refers to:
  □ *What can they tell you about worms?*
  □ *What could the connection be to a book?*
  □ *Does the expression have a similar translation into the language(s) that they speak?*
- Divide the class into small groups of three or four learners.
- Tell the class that you will give each group a list of words or expressions to work with and a time limit (eg of ten minutes) to come up with a meaning for each.
- After the time is up, go through the list and ask each group to tell you what they think the word means:
  □ Award a point to each group that correctly identifies the meaning.
  □ You may want to award points for creativity, even if they are totally wrong.
  □ Explain any unidentified words to the class.
  □ You may want to add more rounds by asking the groups to come up with words of their own to give to their opponents to identify.
- Ask the learners what they call these things in their first language.

Signing off
Ask your class to look out for other unusual or funny expressions that they may come across, and to share these with the class in future lessons.

- daddy long legs
- sleeping policeman
- monkey puzzle
- cat's eye
- milkshake duck
- toadstool
- dog collar (not for dogs)
- mortarboard (not for masonry)
- keyworker

It's gobbledygook to me!

Guessing the meaning of words, using context

Strategy

Deciphering the meaning of words, using contextual clues.

Setting the context

I often advise my learners that, when reading anything in English, they should try not to stop and look up the meaning of every unknown word that they come across but, instead, try to keep reading for gist, and guess its meaning from the clues provided by the context.

Sensible advice, but getting them to do this is easier said than done!

If you are determined to reduce your learners' dependence on translation tools, however, try feeding them nonsense words or 'gobbledygook' (similar to the noise made by a turkey!), so that they have no option but to guess the meaning of the words from the context.

Setting up

Find a text that is appropriate to your learners' level and that you would like to work with. Then select 6–8 words that you would like the learners to guess.

Replace these words with words of your own invention:
- If you struggle to come up with your own words, you could choose translations into a language that the learners are not familiar with.

In the examples below, taken from *A Bear called Paddington* by Michael Bond and *South from Granada* by Gerald Brenan, I have replaced the words in the box on the next page with my own nonsense words.

Step by step

- Give your learners a copy of the text.

- Ask them to read through the text quickly, and underline any words that they do not know.

- Then, depending on the text you have chosen, find example sentences with words which you are sure your learners will already know. Write the sentences on the board, with blanks to replace a few of the familiar words. For example:

    Paddington liked geography. At least, he liked his sort of geography, which meant seeing strange (i) _____ and new (ii) _____.
    (The removed words are: *places* and *people*.)

    Guadix is a (i) _____, noisy, crowded little town with bad (ii) _____ and a large population of very (iii) _____ people.
    (The removed words are: *dirty*, *inns* and *poor*.)

    See the Note below.

- Ask the class:
    - *Is each word a noun, adjective, verb, etc?*
    - *Do the words have any positive or negative connotations?*

- Then ask the learners to suggest words that could fit in the gaps:
    - *How do your learners' suggestions compare to the original words?*

- Tell the class that you would like them to think about the words that they underlined in the text they read:
    - *Can they come up with some alternatives – using any clues that they can find in the text?*

- Ask the class to share their suggestions then, together, compare these with the original words:
    - The learners may also have underlined other words that belong to the original text, but which they did not know.
    - Ask them to tell you what they think these words might mean.

Signing off

Ask your learners about any books that they have read in English, and about their experience doing so:
- *How did they deal with unknown words?*
- *How motivated were they to keep reading?*
- *Did they give up, due to too many unknown words?*

References

Bond, M *A Bear called Paddington* Houghton Mifflin Company 1958

Brenan, G *South from Granada* Hamish Hamilton 1957

Note:

The author of *English is Context* doesn't take responsibility for the opinions of Gerald Brenan, who was writing some time ago.

If you are teaching in Southern Spain, where Guadix is recognised for its cave dwellings, this extract might lead to some lively discussion!

▶▶▶

It's gobbledygook to me!

Paddington was very g'joobed when he woke up the next morning and found himself in bed. He decided it was a nice feeling as he stretched himself and pulled the crabalocker up around his head with a paw. He reached out with his feet and found a cool spot for his toes. One adventure of being a very small bear in a surlaw bed was that there was so much room.

Spring was, as in most countries, the best season. It began on the coast in February or March, and then spread like a stain of green up the crabalocker, reaching the village in April. The fig leaves and mulberry leaves opened, the wheat and the barley g'joobed a little more every night, the surlaw poplar buds unwrapped and delivered their thin, silky sails. The goos arrived and began to build their nests, and before long one heard the cuckoo and the nightingale. Above the village the whole crabalocker was breaking into life.

---

g'joobed – surprised (*A Bear called Paddington*), shot up (*South from Granada*)

crabalocker – sheet (*A Bear called Paddington*), mountain(side) (*South from Granada*)

surlaw – large (*A Bear called Paddington*), sticky (*South from Granada*)

goo – swallow (*South from Granada*)

Something ...

While reading through these chapters, you may have recognised references to songs or lyrics by the Beatles.

The reason for this is manyfold.

Since the beginning of my teaching career:

- ☐ Song lyrics, especially those by John and George, maybe Paul, and probably even Ringo, have been a constant source of my lesson material.
- ☐ The Beatles seem to have followed me around (or perhaps it is me who has followed them?) from Gibraltar (where Lennon got married) to Hamburg (where Lennon famously 'grew up').

But for the purposes of this book, looking at *their* careers can also be a bit like taking a pragmatic mystery tour:

- ☐ From their raw beginnings, playing eight days a week on the Reeperbahn, they were recognised for their twists and shouts.
- ☐ Then they shot to fame, wanting to hold our hand and as we worked it out, love them do.
- ☐ Later, things got more dreamy. Wonderfully ambiguous, they performed for no-one, and encouraged us to find the inner light.
- ☐ Finally, when we were really digging it and they had earned our total respect, they decided to let it be, and go their long and winding roads.

Whether their music is in some way to blame for my love of teaching, or whether it is my teaching that is to blame for my love of their lyrics, I cannot say.

Whatever the case, it has something ... to do with **context**.

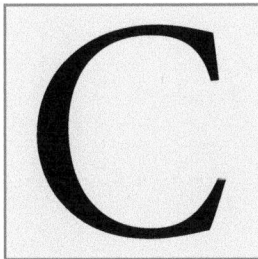

English is Context demonstrates how language – in this case, English – can be interpreted in different ways, depending on the conditions of the situation in which we say things:

- Part A introduced pragmatic competence by taking us on a brief history of discourse – from the etiquette of conversation to speech acts, politeness maxims and the study of linguistic *pragmatics*.
- Part B shared activities for the classroom – to get our learners thinking about how their messages are interpreted, and the implications of what they say – to help them improve their pragmatic *competence*.

Part C will now discuss how *reflecting* on language in context can affect the process of our learners' acquisition of a language in different ways. These are:

Ways to think – with the learner and the *learning* approach in mind.
We reiterate the value of recognising how words work, and the strategies we choose to *communicate* what we want and *get* what we want.

Ways to teach – with the teacher, *teaching* programme and formal assessment in mind.
Here, we compare ways to introduce pragmatics to our curriculum, measuring our learners' competence, and see how official assessment guidelines have been adapted to include pragmatic competence.

Ways to succeed – with the teacher *and* the learner in mind.
We propose an analytical framework for you, the teacher, to refer to in your class planning, and provide your learners with a structure to help them remember what they have learnt and minimise the risk of pragmatic failure – which is no other than '… *the inability to understand 'what is meant by what is said'*'. (Jenny Thomas [1])

From the first step onto the language learning stairway, activities to increase pragmatic awareness may seem like small steps in the learning process.

But each one leads to the next – with the end reward of a higher level of competence – and is, in fact, a giant leap in communicative achievement.

> All the reference numbers in Part C of *English is Context* are fully explained in the Reference section on page 140.

Major levels of linguistic structure

PRAGMATICS
meaning in context
of discourse

SEMANTICS
literal meaning of phrases
and sentences

SYNTAX
phrases and sentences

MORPHOLOGY
words

PHONOLOGY
phonemes

PHONETICS
speech sounds

Adapted from: *Illuminating the Path: The Research and Development Agenda for Visual Analytics* by James Thomas and Kristin Cook [2]

Ways to think – with the learner in mind

'I refuse to believe there isn't any language on the planet where you can't be nice.'
Michael McCarthy [3]

It is far too easy to dismiss a language – or culture – on the basis of how nice (or not) we perceive its speakers to be.

Unless we are satisfied with a superficial stereotype (and the Internet is full of opinionated lists with questionable research into the rudest, angriest, etc) to explain the behaviour of others and how cooperative (or not) we find them to be, we need to look deeper:
- A step in the right direction might be with what we can term 'cross-cultural understanding'.

But, to really open our eyes, the best place to start is with what speakers *intend* to say, and the words that they *choose* to express themselves.

A small step

'The first step, my son, that one takes in the world is the one on which the rest of our lives depends.'
Voltaire [4]

Getting your learners to analyse discourse will not only help them to understand how others communicate, but also help them take a significant first step towards their acquisition of another language:
- Activities that help to increase pragmatic awareness may therefore seem like small advances in the learning process, rather than simply being something that can be inputted clumsily as a coherent theory.

If, for example, we imagine the overall course of language learning as a long stairway to linguistic enlightenment, the very first step to take us there might be the first *sounds* that we make, imitating what we hear.

From this basic grounding, language develops with each step we climb:
- Next comes the *meaning* of words and the *order* in which we use them in a sentence – this seems to be the focus of secondary education, as well as what is required for academic study.
- Subsequently, each step continues to lead to a finer aspect of acquisition, including *context* and how this influences our understanding – ie pragmatic competence.
- Finally, at the top, is a door to linguistic enlightenment.

Although the Thomas and Cook diagram opposite is often shared by language teachers online, it has been argued that pragmatic competence is not a *linguistic* feature:
- But if this is the case, what is it? And does this mean that we shouldn't deal with it in language classes? Absolutely not!

Interestingly, Thomas and Cook were computer scientists, not linguists.

We will impress others with our ability to speak another language, having reached a high knowledge of semantics and syntax – but without taking the *final* step, we may still become lost in interaction with native speakers.

If we think carefully about the question 'How many languages can you speak?' we may struggle to come up with an answer …

What does 'speak' actually *mean*?
- If we already know a few basic phrases and sentences in a language but may struggle to develop conversation …
- Or if we know the words and rules of a language but cannot communicate (see the story of 'Gintas' on page 31 in Part A) …
- Or if we have little awareness of how context can change meaning …

… Are we really being honest if we include these languages in our list of the languages we claim to speak?

This may well be what raises learners from having an 'advanced' level of the language to a higher level that is 'proficient' or 'distinguished' – for want of a better word than 'native', which is often used unfairly and misleadingly by learners and schools.

A 'short and sweet' way to show learners the importance of context might be by giving them phrases like the following, and asking questions about them:

- *Really!?!*
  - Is the speaker who uses this word emphasising conviction – or expressing agreement, surprise, doubt or disagreement?
  - How can the learners tell?
  - What influences their decision?

- *Do you know …?*
  - Does the speaker who is about to give a startling fact expect the hearer to answer 'no'?
  - Or is the question rhetorical?

- *As if!*
  - Is the combination of these two words usually used to express:
    – expectation (*'She behaved as if she had been born in a barn'*)?
    – doubt (*'Ipswich Town promoted? As if!'*)?

- *Fine!*
  - A viral meme reads:
    'Fine doesn't mean *fine*. The scale goes: *great, good, okay, not okay, I hate you, fine.*'

In our daily interactions, we may try to show off with a clever use of wordplay – hoping to amuse, rather than confuse. We do not want the hearer to have to struggle to immediately recognise our wit.

Similarly, Relevance Theory [5] (see 'Relevance in context' on page 28 in Part A) proposes that hearers use contextual clues such as intonation – and stop analysing, as soon as they think they have understood:
- How successfully they do this depends on their level of pragmatic competence.
- The need for such competence depends on our learners' need for the language.

It is usually hoped, both by the speaker *and* the hearer, that we are as 'relevant' as possible.

But what happens when the language we choose to use is not one where the hearer is really adept – where we are unsure of the hearer's ability to understand or even connect?
- Should the speaker still be making the same assumptions?
- Will an ambiguous or sarcastic quip cause amusement – or confusion? For example:
  - *'He says if I don't drink lots of milk, when I grow up I'm only gonna be good enough to play for Accrington Stanley.'* Milk Marketing Board advert, 1989.

I remember when my own use of humour failed to connect in the classroom:
- I fell flat on my metaphorical face, when a learner commented:
  'Sarcasm is not becoming of the English teacher.'

For this reason – before any language teaching can take place – teachers, coursebook writers and syllabus designers now recognise the importance to first identify the learners' *need* for language.

Is it, for example:

- to simply be able to participate in an English-speaking course of further study …
  - where English is the language of instruction, and informal contextual meanings may not be relevant?
- to communicate in their workplace (either locally or in dispersed teams) …
  - where clarity is of economic importance?
- to live in an English-speaking environment …
  - where the learner will be faced with differences in register and inference in daily contexts?
- to work as translators/interpreters …
  - where professionalism depends on an understanding of implicature?

The activities in Part B of this book were created with the above in mind.

A giant leap

'We realise the importance of our voice when we are silenced.'
Malala Yousafzai [6]

An initial step in the direction of further study and reflection of how we – and those we communicate with – choose the words we use to express opinions or feelings, is to also consider how we *accomplish* things (eg gain sympathy, 'fish' for compliments/reassurance, anger or motivate) with these words.

The activities in *English is Context* are aimed at increasing exposure and recognising use.

You might argue that, as learners spend time in an English-speaking environment, they will improve their pragmatic competence anyway:
- But in the Age of Information, where the race is on to produce instant translation tools in combination with devices such as Google's *Pixel Buds* or Apple's *AirPods*, do they have the time or the inclination to do so?
- And what qualifies as an 'English-speaking' environment anyway?

In West African countries where English is the official language, for example, extremely competent teachers who studied the language to university level – but who have not had the chance to spend time in a more affluent English-speaking nation (Britain, Ireland, America, Canada, Australia, New Zealand, etc) – may lack the ability to recognise language in the context of these places and their people:
- Is it fair that they lose credibility with their learners as a consequence?
- How can they help themselves and their learners to overcome this hurdle?

The need to reflect on contextual meaning in language learning is echoed by national and international education boards and their assessment scales, such as the *Common European Framework of Reference for Languages* (CEFR) [7] and the *American Council on the Teaching of Foreign Languages* (ACTFL) [8].

But before we come to exams, we must first consider what can be done in (or – in the case of blended learning – out of) the classroom.

Ways to teach – with the teacher in mind

'Give a man a fish, and you feed him for a day.
Teach a man to fish, and you feed him for a lifetime.'
Anon. [9]

In Part A of this book, we looked at how language teaching has traditionally been prescribed and instructed, rather than being a case of *guided discovery*.

Is it possible that, as teachers, we still spend too much time and effort on feeding our learners what we think they need, to meet language assessment criteria – pronunciation, grammatical structure, vocabulary and collocations, and so on – but overlook how they will survive in that language for the rest of their lives?

This question reminds me of the cautionary tale of the 'wise fool' Nasrudin Hodja, that David Heathfield shared in his book *Storytelling With Our Students* [10].

The story reminds us how such a blind preoccupation with a point of grammar can have catastrophic, as well as 'hilarious', consequences.

The Ferryman and the Grammar Teacher

Nasrudin Hodja was working as a ferryman, rowing people across the wide river in a small boat in exchange for payment.

One day, a grammar teacher came along.

'Will you carry me to the other side?'

'If you pay me.'

'Will the crossing be smooth or rough?' asked the grammar teacher.

'I don't know nothing.'

'I don't know nothing? Have you never learned grammar?'

'No, never.'

'Then you have wasted half of your life!'

Nasrudin Hodja began rowing the grammar teacher across the wide river.

Halfway across, the sky grew dark and the wind began to blow.

A storm broke; there was thunder and lightning.

The waves got bigger and bigger, and started crashing over the side of the small rowing boat.

The boat rocked from side to side – it was certain that it would be turned over.

Nasrudin looked at the grammar teacher, who was holding on to the sides of the boat, terrified.

The colour had drained from his face.

Nasrudin called:

'Have you never learned to swim?'

'No. Never.'

'Then you have wasted all of your life!'

This icon indicates where some of the resources that support and complement Part C have been placed on the DELTA website for you to download for your convenience.

Simply register at www.deltapublishing.co.uk and search for the ISBN 501742 to access the downloadable material.

Learners may be lulled into a false sense of security from being the best at retaining words – and being able to …

- score highly in 'spelling bee' contests;
- memorise lists of irregular verbs;
- recognise the meanings of words that appear in C2-level tests (according to the Common European Framework of Reference for Languages) based on their knowledge of the classics (*funambulist* – from the Latin *funis*, meaning 'rope', and *ambulare*, meaning 'to walk' = 'tightrope walker').

These same learners can be taken aback when thrown into authentic situations and expected to perform 'like a native'.

Isn't it, then, a teacher's responsibility to not just help our learners pass an exam?

A small step

'Sometimes I lie awake at night and I ask "Is life a multiple-choice test or is it a true or false test?" Then a voice comes to me out of the dark and says, "We hate to tell you this but life is a thousand word essay.".'
Charlie Brown [11]

Even a blockhead like Charlie Brown can realise that a top score in a multiple-choice test will not provide sufficient proof of your competence in another language.

Apart from radical educational programmes – such as in Finland's public schools, where there are no standardised tests and only one exam at the end of the senior year in high school – good exam results remain the goal of, perhaps most, educational establishments.

In defence of exams, many will argue that:
- they provide structure;
- they are a measurement of progress;
- they determine if learners are ready for a further level of study.

So, we might wonder, what room is there for increasing pragmatic awareness, when *intake* depends so much on an *input* from beyond the classroom walls?

Fortunately, formal assessment bodies are coming aboard.

There is a noticeable recognition of the importance of contextualised meaning in some of the most dominant official guidelines. Teachers and schools who offer courses or preparation classes according to these criteria will, therefore, be expected to adapt accordingly.

The European Union (in the Common European Framework of Reference for Languages), for example, describes pragmatic competence as being:
- *'concerned with the functional use of linguistic resources (production of language functions, speech acts), drawing on scenarios or scripts of interactional exchanges.'*
and …
- *'the mastery of discourse, cohesion and coherence, the identification of text types and forms, irony, and parody.'* [12]

The framework descriptives for the different levels, however, are perhaps more vague.

At level C1, listeners can:
- *'understand extended speech even when it is not clearly structured and when relationships are only implied and not signalled explicitly.'*
and …

- *'have a good familiarity with idiomatic expressions and colloquialisms'* and express themselves *'fluently and convey finer shades of meaning precisely.'* [13]

Yet, the ways of interpreting phrases such as 'clearly structured' and 'finer shades of meaning' seem correct but clumsy, and open to the examiner's own personal interpretation:

- If contexts always differ and are culturally (in)dependent, the above descriptions suggest that examiners would – biased to their own experience – perhaps base their assessment on a very different setting.
- Would an examiner sent from Northern Europe to assess local ability in Nigeria, for example, first require training in contextual awareness, or can/should there be an absolute?

At lower levels, these seemingly vague expressions become even more open to interpretation.

B1 listeners, for example, are able to *'understand the main point of clear standard speech'* [14].

The focus here suggests a focus on syntax, lexis and pronunciation.

The American Council on the Teaching of Foreign Languages (ACTEFL), on the other hand, doesn't mention pragmatic competence in their guidelines, which are nevertheless much more specific.

To reach a 'distinguished' level of language, users can:

- *'understand a wide variety of forms, styles and registers of speech on highly specialized topics in language that is tailored to different audiences.'*
- understand the language, from classical theatre, art films, professional symposia to *'literary readings, and most jokes and puns.'*
- *'comprehend implicit and inferred information, tone, and point of view, and can follow highly persuasive arguments.'*
- *'understand unpredictable turns of thought related to sophisticated topics.'*
- *'use speech that can be highly abstract, highly technical, or both.'*
- *'comprehend oral discourse that is lengthy and dense, structurally complex, rich in cultural reference, idiomatic and colloquial.'*
  and …
- process *'information that is subtle or highly specialized, as well as the full cultural significance of very short texts with little or no linguistic redundancy'* … and the *'speaker's use of nuance and subtlety.'*

Also …

- *'Their listening ability is enhanced by a broad and deep understanding of cultural references and allusions.'* [15]

In the same report, listeners at the 'Distinguished' level are able to appreciate the richness of the spoken language, and their ability is enhanced by *'a broad and deep understanding of cultural references and allusions'* [16].

Would this mean that the British or Australians who lacked US references are therefore to be considered 'undistinguished'?

On the whole, however, this seems like a very complete description.

Although it is now generally accepted that contextual meaning is vital to master a language by reaching a 'proficient or 'distinguished' level – the testing of pragmatic competence is, itself, fiendishly individual, and open to ambiguity.

A giant leap

'Never again shall a single story be told as though it were the only one.'
John Berger [17]

Attempts to create a situation or context that is relevant to the learners' needs and assesses competence include:
- Carrying out discourse completion tasks:
  - although care needs to be taken that there is no ambiguity in the preceding sentences or description of the context.
- Performing roleplays:
  - although, as we have said earlier in the book, these may fail due to the unnatural conditions.
- Comprehension questions about implicature or register:
  - although this may be highly dependent on the culture, not only of the learner and the speakers, but also of the environment in which the learner will be using the language.

> As you read, you might stop and supply an answer that springs to mind – as if you were a learner who was being asked to respond.

Some examples of the above might be to ask the learner to provide an answer in the situations presented below.

Provide an appropriate and friendly phrase for a given situation.

You are pushed for time and enter a crowded lift. What do you say to the other people in the lift?
Answer: _____ .

Suggested answers: *Please move aside; Is there room for one more?; Excuse me, sorry.*
Inappropriate answers: *Move; I want to come in; the sign says 'This lift carries nine'!*

Check understanding by adding appropriate or friendly phrases to an existing dialogue.

Complete the conversation between a taxi driver and the passenger in the East of England:
Taxi driver: *Hello, luv, where are we off to?*
You: 1 _____ .
Taxi driver: *Sure. Is it alright if we take the back streets to avoid the rush hour traffic?*
You: 2 _____ .

Suggested answers:
1 *The station, please; Sainsbury's; Do you know the bike shop on Woodbridge Road?*
2 *No problem; Of course; I'd rather not; You know best!*
Inappropriate answers:
1 *You're taking me to the College; Sainsbury's, Sweetie.*
2 *Just do what Google (or the satnav) tells you, will you? You're having a laugh!*

Answer multiple-choice questions.

What is the most natural way to respond to the following?
Can you tell me the time?
a) Yes   b) Sure, it's 17:30   c) The time

Appropriate answer: *b)*

Consider the register of a given phrase.

Decide if the following is formal, neutral or informal – and explain your answer:
I cannot thank you enough for everything that you have done on our behalf.

Suggested answer: *The answer is either formal or semi-formal. The speaker does not use any contractions (eg thanks, can't, you've done) and is thanking the hearer on behalf of a group.*

Provide the context of a given phrase.

In what context might you hear the following?
'Do you still have anything electronic, including a mobile phone, with you? If you do, switch it off and give it to one of us now. If you keep any unauthorised items, even if these are in your pockets and you do not intend to use them, you will be disqualified.'

Suggested answer: *An examination room before the start of the test.*

Change the register of a given phrase, so that it is more appropriate for the context.

Rewrite the following in a more appropriate style for a courtroom:
'*... but, no, but, yeah but I know because I'm not wasting police time because you know Micha? Well, she saw the whole thing, right, because she was bunking off school.*'
(Spoken by Vicky Pollard, a comic character from the 'Little Britain' series.)[18]

Suggested answer: *I do not wish to waste police time, Sir/Madam/Your Honour, but would like to inform you that Micha (Surname?) was also witness to the event, due to not attending school that day.*

As examination questions, none of the above can be said to be completely failproof.

The difficulty is that there can only ever be *suggested* answers, and, as far as pragmatic competence is concerned, room must also be made for 'unexpected answers':
- In the case of the taxi driver above, the following may not be immediately apparent:
  - *I've cut my finger.*
  - *My husband is just locking the door.*

For the moment, at least, such answers:
- will need 'expert' knowledge to determine whether they are to be considered 'correct';
- cannot be graded by a machine or by Artificial Intelligence.

Context, as this book aims to demonstrate, is highly *specific* and prone to many *variables* – eg the hierarchy, age, sex, belief, culture, location, intimacy, etc, of the speakers:
- With each of the above, there should therefore be a number of follow-up questions to determine the exact context and what is *inappropriate*, and what *incorrect*.
- For example, after the question:
  'What differences can you assume between the passenger and driver?'
  A suggested answer could be: *The passenger is of the opposite sex to the driver and there is an age difference between the two.*
- Besides, while it might be easier to decide which answers are a 'pragmatic failure', there will be a number of situations that can be taken into consideration.

Each activity in this book encourages the learner to bear in mind that:
- there is often no single solution or right way to communicate;
- planning an appropriate response can be a waste of time;
- contextual differences can threaten ability to communicate.

Acquiring pragmatic competence is, therefore, a continual process of reflection, not only by the *learner* but also the *teacher*, on what we discover *together*.

It is important that *both* are regularly encouraged to share their experiences of how and when they put these discoveries into practice, to help the class to succeed in what is an increasingly unpredictable world.

Ways to succeed – with teacher and learner in mind

'Hey, it's crazy out there!'
Nathan Bennett and G. James Lemoine [19]

At the end of the twentieth century – when the status quo of 'East versus West' collapsed, with the fall of a concrete wall – Eastern Europe spoke of 'Awakenings' (and Velvet and Orange Revolutions, in Czechoslovakia and Ukraine, etc), as they started to revolt against communism.

Later, the Arab world had their 'Springs'.

Claims for renewed independence toppled regimes, and new deals were struck by former enemies, who were 'cautiously optimistic' and could 'do business together' – in the words of the then UK Prime Minister Margaret Thatcher [20].

A complex new order of intertwined relationships between nations suddenly began to take shape.

To describe that new world, the US military proposed VUCA:

Volatility – Uncertainty – Complexity – Ambiguity

A 'horrible acronym', as one *Financial Times* reporter called it [21], the term was soon adopted by management gurus as a trendy word to explain the complexities of the business world in the 21st Century – a volatile world:
- where anything that could happen probably would;
- where relationships between businesses were no longer as black and white as they once seemed, but far more uncertain and complex than ever;
- where success depended on how well they sustained themselves, their reputation, and their ability to recognise ambiguity.

Two decades into a new millennium, we do not seem to have got any better.

As the world battles a prospect of several waves of a pandemic, things seem more complex – each day bringing a need to adjust to change, in preparation for not just a new 'normal' but potential *normals*.

Or shall we call them 'contexts'?

A small step

'Complications arose, ensued, were overcome.'
Captain Jack Sparrow [22]

As far as languages go, English may appear to be disordered, maybe even anarchic:
- The spelling is definitely *awkward* – 'awkward' with two *w*s being just one example. (See the activity on autological words (*A word is a word – or is it?*) on page 60.)
- The pronunciation is never as *thorough* as one might have *thought* – for example, 'ough', can be pronounced eight different ways in American English, nine in British English.
- Often, adverbs of time can *often* appear anywhere within a clause … *often*.
- And *going on* to verb patterns – verbs followed by gerunds or the *to*-infinitive *go on* confusing the language learner. We could *go on*!

In truth, it is incredibly complex.

There are no *rules* for how to imply things with words which:
- appear to be the same but contradict themselves (eg to start a clock or to end a business by *winding them up*; to remove an excess of hair or to add to the decoration of a Christmas tree by *trimming it*).
- appear contradictory to one another but which have the same, or very similar, meanings (*a slim chance* and *a fat chance*; *a care taker* and *a care giver*; *quite a lot* and *quite a few*).
- contradict themselves in the same compound (*random order*; *deafening silence* – for more oxymorons, see the activity *Brutally civil* on page 118).

To understand meaning, therefore, we can only recognise the expectations – in the hope that the speaker will be cooperative, and that hearers are competent enough to process our message.

Language shows no mercy. It's just not cricket!

The rules of cricket
The ins and outs

You have two sides, one out in the field and one in.

Each man who is in the side that's in goes out, and when he's out he comes in and the next man goes in until he's out.

When they are all out, the side that's out comes in, and the side that's been in goes out and tries to get those coming in out.

Sometimes you get men still in and not out.

When a man goes out to go in, the men who are out try to get him out, and when he is out he goes in and the next man in goes out and goes in.

There are two men called umpires who stay out all the time and they decide when the men who are in are out.

When both sides have been in and all the men have been out, and both sides have been out twice after all the men have been in, including those who are not out, that is the end of the game.

A giant leap

' "No, I don't suffer from freckles," said Pippi.
Then the lady understood, but she took one look at Pippi and burst out,
"But, my dear child, your whole face is covered with freckles!"
"I know it," said Pippi, "but I don't suffer from them. I love them." '
From 'Pippi Longstocking' – Astrid Lindgren [23]

To help our learners take stock of what they have already learnt, and make sense of the unpredictability of context, perhaps we need look no further than VUCA.

In an attempt to make the acronym more approachable, Bill George of the Harvard Business School proposed an updated 2.0 version [24]:

Vision – Understanding – Courage – Adaptability

Perhaps these words are too simplistic and superficial to describe the complexities of today's world, but they do seem to summarise the generally accepted merits of a language learner.

To satisfy our needs in this book, however, I suggest one further change:

Vibe – Unpredictability – Challenge – Application

VUCA ELT does not assume to be a teaching method, nor does it suggest ways to adapt materials. It is intended as nothing more than an awareness guideline when preparing learners to *expect*, and even be part of, the *unexpected* – when communicating in English.

Vibe

Defined by the online *Oxford Advanced Learners Dictionary* as 'a mood or an atmosphere produced by a particular person, thing or place' [25]. In our case, the 'vibe' determines the words that we choose to express ourselves, how we use these words, and the linguistic strategies that we adopt to achieve our wants and aims.

When speakers enter into conversation, we make a semi-conscious decision about the words to use, based on our relationship to the hearer(s):
- whether we know them well, or whether they are strangers;
- how their position compares to ours within a hierarchy or society;
- knowing the differences between their and our cultural backgrounds.

All provide important clues to what is appropriate – but the speakers also need to know what is considered right for the *situation*.

When will cracking a joke or swearing at a funeral endear us to, rather than alienate us from, the congregation? See John Cleese's eulogy to Graham Chapman at his memorial service, for example, where he says:
'Good riddance to him, the freeloading bastard! I hope he fries.' [26]

Those who are familiar with John Cleese may already be smiling as they read these words.

To be pragmatically competent, we need to seize the moment with the ability to 'pick up the vibe', using the social or environmental clues that we need to interact naturally with others.

A failure to connect with the situation can mean that our message, or the message given by others, is misunderstood – leading to breakdown in communication, and an atmosphere that is tense, or possibly even hostile.

Unpredictability

In many of the activities in Part B, learners are caught off-guard by examples of unexpected responses in conversations, and how the meanings of words and phrases depend on the contexts in which they are used.

The author's personal introduction to this book compared language to driving a car – just like in traffic, knowing how others will behave, respond and react depends entirely on the individual and his or her *circumstance*:
- The difficulty with training in pragmatic competence is the uniqueness of each and every situation, and the unpredictability of others within it.

The situations imagined and simulated in the language learning classroom are stereotypical and rely on certain conditions being true. Such a simplification can lead to an over-reliance on those conditions and consequent failure in perhaps very similar *situations* – but with very different *speakers* and *backgrounds*.

To have a good level of competence, it is important to remember not to attempt to simplify and expect, but to be ready for the challenge that each new situation presents.

Challenge

An experience often shared by workers in the offices of international companies is the one when the phone rings and displays a '00' prefix, indicating a call from abroad. Everybody pretends to be too busy to answer – in the hope that somebody else will pick up.

Interacting with others, no matter what the language of communication, in such a public place poses an on-the-spot test of not just *ability*, but the challenge for the receiver to make immediate *decisions* about the words and the register to use, and the strategies which will help to 'connect' with the caller – for a friendly, natural conversation to take place.

Recognising the relationship to the hearer will determine the familiarity, and – depending on what they both hope to achieve and the level of imposition – will determine the strategies they will use to get what they want.

The choices we make about how to communicate can rarely be planned in advance, and may change unexpectedly at any time. Success, therefore, can only be decided if we are ready to accept the challenge in the first place.

Application

English is Context only scratches the surface of the many strategies of politeness and impoliteness theory; flouts Grice's [27] and Leech's [28] maxims (see pages 20–23 in Part A); and plays around with the very conditions that speech acts depend on – but all of these are simply *observations*: there may be *expectations*, but no *rules* for our behaviour.

To understand how we use the language(s) we speak – what works and with whom – can be a continual process of trial and error, facing 'unknown unknowns', experimenting by *applying* and *adjusting* what we have learnt and are comfortable with.

A colleague and friend, Hannah Shipman, said: *'This is a fascinating area. To what extent can I – as a teacher – keep my identity when interacting with learners? How 'authentic' should I be with my interactions and language? What is appropriate? It's hard and it's fun.'*

VUCA ELT gives method to the madness, reasons to that which may seem unreasonable, and provides structure to that which seems unstructured.

'The greatest teacher failure is.'
Yoda [29]

Encouraging learners to share their stories of how they, or others, pragmatically failed when attempting to use language in a real-life context will open a can of worms – each example releasing a bunch of experiences, with learners learning from one another.

As they do, the role of the *teacher* changes to one of a *guide* – leading the class in their linguistic exploration.

The discoveries you will make together on the way say as much about you and the language you are trying to teach as about the learners themselves – as, in the process, they climb from *competent* to *distinguished*: to a higher and broader awareness of language.

And rather than speaking dismissively of 'failures', you can help your learners focus on what they have already learnt from the experience, and how they can *succeed* … pragmatically!

In *English is Context*, we have seen the incredible diversity of the English language – and that, by *context*, we mean:
- the speakers;
- their relationship to one another;
- their environment;
- the time at which the language is used.

It should be noted that this book was written at an extremely volatile time: one of dissatisfaction with world leaders and authorities, when the fear of having destroyed our environment beyond repair was at its greatest yet, and during which the fury of a global pandemic forced the global village to socially isolate itself.

Yet there is now a glimmer of hope.

With the Internet:
- 'communities' are larger than has ever been possible;
- solidarity with our neighbours is seeing a new dawn;
- a shared concern for the earth has led to a global 'youthquake'.

It is impossible to say how such a fickle world will affect how we communicate in the future.

To write a book at a time of such constant and rapid change has not been easy.

While this author may be quick to sympathise with Huck Finn when he completed *his* own book, it has also been an exciting and eye-opening challenge to write about the role of constantly evolving context(s) – as we modify and adapt our language learning and, ultimately, our teaching:
- by providing resources which attempt to understand the behaviour of others, as well as ourselves, through linguistic observation;
- by suggesting ways for the learners of the language to make sense of the uncertainty of the future.

Perhaps there has been no better occasion to complete what I would describe – in *my* own words – as something that 'seemed like a good idea at the time'.

> ' … and so there ain't nothing more to write about,
> and I am rotten glad of it, because if I'd a knowed what a trouble
> it was to make a book I wouldn't a tackled it,
> and ain't a-going to no more.'
>
> Huckleberry Finn [30]

References

1 Thomas, J 'Cross-cultural pragmatic failure' *Applied Linguistics* 4 (2) 1983

2 Thomas, J J and Cook, K A (Eds) 'Illuminating the Path: The Research and Development Agenda for Visual Analytics' National Visualization and Analytics Center 2005

3 McCarthy, M 'How can a corpus help us organise advanced level teaching?' Plenary: Cambridge Exams Centre DE007/HELTA, delivered 25 January 2020

4 Voltaire *L'Indiscret* Act I, Scene I, Chez Noël Pissot … et François Flahault 1725
(Translation of the original: 'Le premier pas, mon fils, que l'on fait dans le monde est celui dont dépend le reste de nos jours.')
Digitised Oxford University 26 March 2007

5 Wilson, D and Sperber, D 'Relevance Theory' *UCL Psychology and Language Sciences* (Paper available as a pdf) 2002
Sperber, D and Wilson D *Relevance: Communication and Cognition* Harvard University Press 1986

6 Yousafzai, M Speech at the Youth Takeover of the United Nations, delivered 12 July 2013

7 Council of Europe 'Common European Framework of Reference for Languages: Learning, Teaching, Assessment' (CFER) Cambridge University Press 2001

8 *American Council on the Teaching of Foreign Languages* 'ACTEFL Proficiency Guidelines' ACTFL, Inc 2012

9 A highly contested quote, possibly attributable to the Chinese philosopher Lao Tzu, founder of Taoism. The oldest English-language use of the proverb has been found in Anne Isabella Thackeray Ritchie's novel *Mrs. Dymond* (1885), in a slightly different form: '[…] if you give a man a fish he is hungry again in an hour. If you teach him to catch a fish you do him a good turn.' (Wikiquote)

10 Heathfield, D *Storytelling With Our Students* DELTA Publishing 2014

11 Schulz, C M 'I told you so, you blockhead' United Feature Syndicate 1999

12 Council of Europe 'Common European Framework of Reference for Languages: Learning, Teaching, Assessment' (*op. cit.*)

13 *Ibid.*

14 *Ibid.*

15 *American Council on the Teaching of Foreign Languages* ACTEFL Proficiency Guidelines 2012 (*op. cit.*)

16 *Ibid.*

17 Berger, J *G.* Weidenfeld & Nicolson 1972

18 *Little Britain* BBC television series 2003–2005

19 Bennett, N and Lemoine, G J 'What VUCA really means for you' *Harvard Business Review* January–February 2014

20 Cole, J Interview with Margaret Thatcher BBC 1984

21 Skapinker, M 'The empty consolation of "Vuca" and other buzzwords'
Financial Times October 23, 2018 https://www.ft.com/content/9aa465fe-d5e7-11e8-ab8e-6be0dcf18713

22 Bruckheimer, J (Producer) & Verbinski, G (Director) *Pirates of the Caribbean: Dead Man's Chest*: Walt Disney Pictures / Jerry Bruckheimer Films 2006

23 Lindgren, A *Pippi Långstrump går ombord* Rabén & Sjögren 1946
Translated: Lindgren, A *Pippi Goes Aboard* Oxford University Press 2002

24 George, B, 'VUCA 2.0: A Strategy For Steady Leadership In An Unsteady' World 2017
https://www.forbes.com/sites/hbsworkingknowledge/2017/02/17/vuca-2-0-a-strategy-for-steady-leadership-in-an-unsteady-world/#3045f59d13d8

25 'Vibes' Oxford Learners Dictionaries Oxford University Press 2020 https://www.oxfordlearnersdictionaries.com/definition/english/vibes?q=vibe

26 Cleese, J and Chapman, G (deceased) Memorial Service, Great Hall at St. Bartholomew's Hospital, London, October 6, 1989
https://www.youtube.com/watch?v=CkxCHybM6Ek

27 Grice, P 'Logic and conversation' In Cole, P and Morgan, J (Eds) *Syntax and Semantics 3 – Speech acts* New York: Academic Press 1975

28 Leech, G *Principles of Pragmatics* Longman Group Ltd 1983

29 Kennedy, K and Bergman, R (Producers), Johnson, R (Director) *Star Wars: The Last Jedi*: Lucasfilm Ltd 2017

30 Twain, M *Adventures of Huckleberry Finn* University of California Press 1985 (First published 1884)

From the editors

English is Context sets off with the words of Spanish philosopher José Ortega y Gasset: *'I am me and my circumstance'*.

I am my context.

Unlike many books that support teachers in their pedagogical journey, the content of *English is Context* is inseparable from the author and *his* context.

This perhaps allows this page 'from the editors' to follow Andreas's example and, for once, leave behind the neutral, impartial commentary on another 'book for teachers'.

As teachers ourselves, we can, for once, speak in the first person and can openly admit to a huge empathy with, and understanding of, the author and his 'first personalisation' of the content of *English is Context*.

Part A offers theory: spreading its net wide – from the author's personal perspectives, through a history of language over the ages, quoting the most surprising of references, to the language classroom: and the English language classroom in particular.

Part B offers activities: a first set of 'mini' activities to open our eyes to what the author considers one of the best-kept secrets of language teaching and learning: *pragmatics*; and a second set that investigates the importance of context in the language we use, before delving deeper into how we speak, and the many ways we *say* – or don't say – what we may – or may not – *mean*!

Part C offers reflection: how to relate the issue of pragmatics to the teacher, to the learner and, ultimately, to both together – in a way that a greater, shared, discovery of what is *pragmatic competence* is succcessfully achieved.

English is Context is as enjoyable to read as it will be enjoyable to teach. It is amusing, yet with authority; provocative, yet without giving offence; unexpected, yet with clarity.

English is Context helps teachers and, what is hugely important, helps their students to really understand – through English *in* context – how English *is* context.

Mike Burghall
Lindsay Clandfield

From the publisher

DELTA TEACHER DEVELOPMENT SERIES

A pioneering, multi-award-winning series of books for English Language Teachers with professional development in mind, blending theory, practice and development.

Teaching Unplugged
Dogme in English Language Teaching
by Scott Thornbury
ISBN: 9783125013582

The Developing Teacher
Practical activities for professional development
by Duncan Foord
ISBN: 9783125013582

Being Creative
The challenge of change in the classroom
by Chaz Pugliese
ISBN: 9783125013513

Teaching Online
Tools and techniques, options and opportunities
by Nicky Hockly and Lindsay Clandfield
ISBN: 9783125013551

Culture in our Classrooms
Teaching language through cultural content
by Gill Johnson and Mario Rinvolucri
ISBN: 9783125013643

The Business English Teacher
Professional principles and practical procedures
by Debbie Barton, Jennifer Burkart and Caireen Sever
ISBN: 9783125013520

Digital Play
Computer games and language aims
by Kyle Mawer and Graham Stanley
ISBN: 9783125013599

The Book of Pronunciation
Proposals for a practical pedagogy
by Jonathan Marks and Tim Bowen
ISBN: 9783125013605

The Company Words Keep
Lexical chunks in language teaching
by Paul Davis and Hanna Kryszewska
ISBN 9783125013575

From the publisher

DELTA TEACHER DEVELOPMENT SERIES

For more information, visit the DTDS website at:
www.deltapublishing.co.uk

Spotlight on Learning Styles
Teacher strategies for learner success
by Marjorie Rosenberg
ISBN: 9783125013636

The Autonomy Approach
Language learning in the classroom and beyond
Brian Morrison and Diego Navarro
ISBN: 9783125013650

Storytelling With Our Students
Techniques for telling tales from around the world
by David Heathfield
ISBN: 9783125013544

Going Mobile
Teaching with hand-held devices
by Nicky Hockly and Gavin Dudeney
ISBN: 9783125013537

Film in Action
Teaching language using moving images
by Kieran Donaghy
ISBN: 9783125013667

Teaching Lexically
Principles and practice
by Hugh Dellar and Andrew Walkley
ISBN: 9783125013612

Teaching English as a Lingua Franca
The journey from EFL to ELF
by Marek Kiczkowiak and Robert J. Lowe
ISBN: 9783125017351

YOUNG LEARNERS

Teaching children how to learn
Plan, Do, Review
by Gail Ellis and Nayr Ibrahim
ISBN: 9783125013629

Teaching English to Pre-Primary Children
Educating very young children
by Sandie Mourão with Gail Ellis
ISBN 9783125013995